This book is dedicated to my parents for their continual love and support. Thank you mom & dad, I love you both.

I'd like to give a special thank you to Cathy, Charlie, Sean, and my dad for sharing your time with me and supporting this endeavor.

Finally I'd like to give a very special thank you to Shannon who spent considerable time and energy to make this readable. You're the best. Lunch is on me.

entrepreneurs

start up

Entrepreneurs are fighters, and they're scrappy, and they're tough, and they're resilient. They are the people who wake up every day to forge their own destiny. But they're also human, and they have fears, and they have flaws, and they make mistakes. And sometimes they fall down. I wanted to share stories from successful entrepreneurs who maybe weren't always successful at everything. Entrepreneurs, who put it on the line and took a risk despite all the people in the world who said they would fail. And perhaps part of their drive to succeed is to prove those people wrong.

Being successful at anything takes constant work. Being a successful entrepreneur requires all of that and more. It takes discipline, dedication, leadership, teamwork, and long hours. Sometimes it's easy to forget entrepreneurs are also people. They're people with families, and friends, and lives outside of their work. They have families to eat dinner with, or spouses to go on vacation with, or kids to take to school. They have friends they spend time with and hobbies they are passionate about. All of the ways people choose to spend their time throughout the week, or month become much more valued and precious to an entrepreneur. It's rare that they are able to spare a moment and share their thoughts and experiences with the world.

So this is a book for, and about entrepreneurial leaders. That's the hope at least. I wanted to document some of their stories, and some of their experiences that

entrepreneurs

have helped them succeed, or trying times that provided hard learned lessons. I wanted to share some of their wisdom because small business owners are an important part of our society. They are continually building upon, creating, and accumulating wealth beyond financial gain. In short: they're improving the world.

Collectively entrepreneurs own a vast wealth of knowledge and experience. They have stories that can make you laugh, or cry, or feel inspired to change the world. They can provide mentorship and guidance that can improve your decision making, or provide a different perspective. I managed to sit down with a few very supportive people who were kind enough to spend time sharing some of their stories with me. Four people who have never meet one another, but who share one common trait: they're entrepreneurs.

I wanted to share not only their successes, but also some of their failures. There are many anecdotes shared by the uber successful about how they failed at 10 business before the succeeded at one. However I feel this only pays lip service to how valuable failure can be. The tacit knowledge we gain in failure helps shape who we are. It's the failures we don't learn from that hold us back. Personal failings can translate into professional failure when we don't grow beyond our current limits. Professional failure can lead to a collapse of our personal lives when we allow those mistakes to consume us.

I also wanted to write a different kind of book that talked about business and leadership. There are many very wonderful books that discuss business or leadership they are often written in one of two formats. The first is

entrepreneurs

the instructional manual. Do these 10 things and your life will be amazing; you'll get to live the American dream that every entrepreneur believes in. All you have to do is follow this step by step instruction. Some of these instructional manuals are written from the first person perspective. Filled with anecdotes from successful business leaders who correlate their success with a certain strategy or particular leadership trait that you should emulate. They give examples of commonly held beliefs on successful business practices for leveraging capital or improving your cash flow cycle. Millions of people have utilized these how to guides and achieved their own success. The information those types of books contain can provide good direction, and introduce some foundational knowledge critical for success, and they cover topics like leadership, money management, and strategy.

    The second type of book is generally the extreme success story. Books about people like Elon Musk and his rise with Tesla, or Mark Zuckerberg and the creation of Facebook, or Jeff Bezos who started Amazon by selling books out of his garage and grew it into the Amazon we know and love today. It's the billionaires club. They have engaging, and often suspenseful stories. Dramatic stories filled with struggles, and failures that take the reader on an adventure that ultimately leads to their breakout success. These books are extremely inspirational and those people should be admired for what they have accomplished. They represent the pinnacle of capitalism. They're also extremely rare.

    With this book I wanted to focus on what 99% of all businesses in the United States are: small businesses (as

entrepreneurs

defined by the SBE council)[1]. There are close to 30 million small businesses in the United States, and the majority of people who open a business are going to open a restaurant, or a hair salon, or a dry cleaner, or a mechanic's shop. They probably won't become billionaires. Though they absolutely could. Maybe they will be one of the few individuals that will open their business at the right time, with the right idea, and they'll make all the right decisions. Maybe you're reading this right now sitting across from the next person who will reshape the technology industry. A fatalist might say there's no stopping them. Regardless, I would never try to discourage someone from chasing their dreams (although I might offer some measured advice to have a plan).

However, the bravest, smartest, strongest, savviest entrepreneurs will most likely not become the next billionaires. More than likely they'll provide for their families. They'll run a successful business, pay their bills, provide jobs in their communities, contribute positively to society, and be perfectly happy. And they should be happy because that is what success looks like. Dave Chappelle once said, *"if I can make a teacher's salary doing comedy, I think that's better than being a teacher."*[2] That quote truly captures what it means to be an entrepreneur. Most entrepreneurs believe if they can make a living by starting a business, it's better than working for someone else. It's better than just earning a paycheck. Entrepreneurship represents passion for living life well. It is the notion that

---

[1] Visit http://sbecouncil.org/about-us/facts-and-data/ for more information about the small business statistics

[2] This is from Dave Chappelle's 2006 interview with James Lipton on Inside the Actor's Studio

entrepreneurs

living life is more than climbing a corporate ladder. It's the belief that a human life deserves more than a death by cubical.

    I also felt it was important to include how each person's story impacted me and how I interpreted some of the things that were discussed. My hope is that the takeaways I provide offer up a good starting place for your own internal monologue. My hope for you, the reader, is that you also see the value in hearing first hand accounts from various people and can pull, and distill your own thoughts and feelings about each experience shared here. The goal here is to present information in a digestible format so that you can ultimately form your own roadmap to success.

    In these sections I discuss some common leadership, and entrepreneur themes that I identified as I re-listened to, and re-read the interviews. However don't mistake these summaries as a "lessons learned" or a how-to compendium. These commentaries shouldn't be viewed as the end-all-be-all formula for success in leadership, or entrepreneurship. Rather they are how I interpreted the information contained within from a lens of the topics I find professionally relevant or personally interesting. If nothing else each story might to stimulate your own internal discussion. There's are an infinite number of ways to examine each experience and my hope is that the stories below add value for you in someway as you travel down your own path towards success.

    If you are reading this at a time far removed from the date of publication, I want to give you some context as to the social and political landscape in which these stories

entrepreneurs

were collected. I suspect things will be very different in 2119 than they are in 2019.

It should also be noted the interviews ahead are not captured verbatim. While the stories are from real people who started and own real businesses, most people don't speak in a text-ready format, especially in an off-the-cuff setting. As with any natural conversation, there is a rapport that develops between the two speakers. Humans tend to use a lot of ums, likes, and other verbal cues that don't translate well into written format. Some of the most common are the use of "right" or "you know" as a way to confirm engagement in the conversation. A back and forth acknowledgement between each speaker responding to rhetorical questions and other nonverbal social cues. Much of that was removed. We also tend to repeat ourselves or stutter start sentences which can be confusing to read. And sometimes the syntax of a verbal statement is contextually understood but appears awkward or clunky in writing.

There were also some interesting side stories I wanted to capture that felt I should be organized into spots where they made more sense. I'm pretty clumsy when I speak, so some of the questions I ask are not posed as gracefully as you might read them. As a result, a lot of time was spent ensuring the reader would be able to clearly grasp the ideas being conveyed by each person being interviewed.

To be clear: 100% of the ideas, concepts, and beliefs are those of the individuals represented ahead. I wanted you, the reader, to be able to immerse yourself in the content and in the conversations. That is difficult to

entrepreneurs

achieve when adding (words), or [paraphrases], or ... to every paragraph. So, even though each chapter accurately reflects the thoughts, opinions, and beliefs each person presented at the time of the interview, it is probably around 85% their exact words, and 15% editorial discretion. This is also not an exposé piece or investigative journalism. I wanted to represent the people I interviewed accurately but also positively; while focusing specifically on the goals of this piece – capturing their entrepreneurial journey.

So those are the objective descriptions of the content ahead, a couple of disclaimers, and a bit of the mechanical process for translating verbal communication into a readable format. All of which is important to get a clearer picture of each set of circumstances, and to better understand each person as human, not a set of sentences strung together about them.

Hopefully in reading their stories of both their successes and failures you feel more connected with your community. If one person can feel more sympathetic to the people around them, or more engaged with their peers, or provide them with comfort or inspiration, I will consider this book a success. I hope you enjoy reading their stories as much as I do.

entrepreneurs

Cathy Oskowiak: Foster Angles on Earth, Inc.

　　I think the spirit to carry on has been a common theme among every business owner I've spoken with and Cathy most definitely has that. Cathy is one of the most caring people I know. She has more love in her heart than anyone I've ever met, and she shares it with all of her friends and family.

　　To give some background, I met Cathy through my former life in roller derby. She was already doing a million things with her life but she wanted a hobby where she could skate, and where it was socially acceptable to hit people. Roller derby fit that nicely. I know I opened by touting Cathy's overflowing compassion but as you'll read throughout this interview and the following chapters, if you're going to be an entrepreneur, you're going to have a little edge somewhere. Eventually, both of us moved away from derby for different reasons but we kept in contact through social media. More than three years later I was in a grocery store in Flourtown, PA, and when I looked up from an open cooler, there was Cathy. I wasn't sure if it was her, but I blurted out her name. I figured if it wasn't her, the worst that would happen is a suburbanite mom would think I was a weirdo.

　　We spent about 15 minutes chatting and catching up. I remembered she had a Christmas charity she organized every year and when I asked about it she told me she had turned it into a real life non-profit. I knew immediately I wanted her to be a part of this project. If nothing else, I wanted to shine some light on what she

entrepreneurs

does. And if one more person knows about Foster Angles on Earth[3] I'll be happy because I think it's a great cause and it addresses a need within our community. I also have a personal attachment to the foster community: my mom and two of my uncles were adopted.

The foundation she started is categorized as a 501(c)(3) organization, or colloquially: a non-profit. For the budding entrepreneur seeking to turn a passion project into a business venture, you will read about Cathy and the story of how she turned her passion for helping children in need into tangible results. You'll read how that passion inspired her to dedicate countless hours and organize hundreds of people over a decade's long charity she grew into a non-profit.

To begin, I'd like to outline the few differences that separate a non-profit organization from a typical business. The first being the 510(c)(3) designation. This comes directly from IRS tax code. It is distinctly separate from a charity in that it is by all rights defined as a corporation and is required to have articles of incorporation, a charter, and generally must have a minimum of 3 distinct board members. Operating a non-profit is a little bit different than operating a business. A business exists to earn profits. You are spending money with the expectation that you'll make money.

But don't mistake non-profit for non-revenue. A non-profit must still generate revenue. Often this is accomplished by fundraising or donations or charity work. The difference comes with how that revenue is utilized. As

---

[3] For more information about Foster Angles on Earth, go to www.FostereAngelsOnEarth.com or contact Cathy@FosterAngelsOnEarth.com

entrepreneurs

the name implies, rather than deriving a profit from revenue earned, the revenue that is generated is used to create value for the community in some way. Instead creating value by making more money with those investment dollars, you're creating value for your investors because their interests align with your interests. Often, stakeholder value in the non-profit sector can't be quantified in the way people like to see: with dollars and cents. And so the challenge becomes how to translate the impact of the mission has within the community or the value the mission adds to people's lives.

    I also wanted to open with Cathy's interview because it was done in December of 2017. Foster Angles had officially incorporated in March of 2017. Cathy filed the organization's first quarterly taxes in July. She was less than a year into this adventure when we spoke, and still in the thick of the startup phase. She faced unexpected struggles, she generated some small wins, and she wanted to quit. Less than one year into starting her organization, she was ready to throw in the towel.

    Entrepreneurs are scrappy by nature, and the few who decide to found non-profits are scrappy with a serious dose of heart. This describes Cathy quite well so I hope you can relate to the excitement and enthusiasm she has for her new endeavor. It certainly is representative of what it means to be an entrepreneur. Passion, dedication, doubts, fears, all mixed in with the belief that she is going to do something great.

entrepreneurs

ɸ

Carlos: I like doing these interviews in a casual setting. It's uncomfortable to be in a room just staring at someone one on one. When it's in public there's background noise, normal conversation going on. There's food, there's drink. It brings some normalcy to a situation a lot of people aren't comfortable with. But let's start off with basic introductions. Your name is?

Cathy Oskowiak: *Cathy Oskowiak.*

Carlos: And you started a non-profit group. Would you care to share?

Cathy Oskowiak: *Our non-profit is Foster Angels on Earth. We kind of evolved into that. It's a non-profit organization that benefits foster children. Our goal is to try to provide some of the things necessary to meet their some of their daily basic needs. To make their lives a little bit easier while they're in care for both the foster children and the homes they are entering.*

We started about ten years ago as a charity. It was just a Christmas charity to start off with, and over the course of those ten years and helping thousands of kids at Christmas time, I began to realize there was a much greater need in the system than just a toy at Christmas. So I've started working with an adoption worker to kind of bring this into the mainstream. Bring awareness about what the gaps in the system there actually are. And that's what we're trying to address. Helping the kids meet more of their day to day needs. It'll be more than just presents at Christmastime. That's what we're going to start doing.

Carlos: And just to give a little bit more description for the readers, this is brand new, right? You've been doing this

entrepreneurs

as a passion and a hobby for ten years, the actual non-profit organization and structure have been in place for about how long? When did you file your paperwork?

Cathy Oskowiak: *Not even a whole year. February, so we're coming up on, I think we're in month ten right now. February is when we decided to incorporate. And that's when we hired the lawyer and we really started the paperwork process.*

We had to start with the articles of incorporation and our motto and all the other structural things like building our board. And then once that was all in place we had to become an official business through the state, so we did that process and then after that we had to submit for federal approval. I wanna say this July I had to file my first tax return for the quarter, and we'd only really been in business for like three months so, we didn't really have much going on.

Carlos: So July was the end of your first quarter. Actually let me circle back here a little bit to some of the things we were discussing earlier. Did you start doing this before or after you adopted your son?

Cathy Oskowiak: *After. Yeah. Adopting my son from foster care was kind of the catalyst for all of this; for the Christmas charity, for the non-profit. That's what introduced me to the system that I had no idea about. I mean I had a little bit of an idea because I was a pediatric nurse at St. Chris, but it really opened the doors wide once we adopted him. We got to see an entirely different side of this underserved section of our society.*

Carlos: So you're going through the adoption process. You learn how the system works and then you decide to start

entrepreneurs

the charity. For ten years. It started as a hobby or a passion I guess is a better description. What changed over that ten years that made you want to take that next step? When did you decide to make this a full-blown non-profit? That's a big step because it's basically like going from selling cookies at a bake sale to forming a corporation and competing with Mrs. Fields.

Cathy Oskowiak: *When we started out, when it was just the Christmas event, I was a Girl Scout leader. So I had actually made it our charity event for the year. And then we just kind of kept doing it every year. And it kept growing every year. We started with 50 kids the first year and last year there were 450 kids. So it was growing and growing.*

As the event became bigger and bigger, I got to know the people at the agency where we adopted our son because that's who we were partnering with. They knew I was a pediatric nurse, they knew I had a passion for helping others, and so they asked me if I would be willing to help them throughout the year training foster parents. So I started doing some training classes for foster parents. Every foster parent has to do so many hours of training to ensure they can meet basic care needs. So I agreed, and I started doing that, and I would teach at different classes. Mostly I would teach what's called a medical treatment course; any foster kid with a medical issue is a medical treatment child. Once a medical treatment child came into service, I would be responsible to go out to the home and teach the foster parent how to take proper care of these children. For example if a child needs insulin shots a foster parent would need medical training on how to administer those, but also recognize basic symptoms, what questions

entrepreneurs

to ask. All of the things a parent would learn. So after doing a number of these medical treatment classes I ended up, well I guess I'd say they suckered me into doing a little bit more and a little bit more. So of course we eventually we ended up fostering some kids which is always emotional. Good but emotional.

It started with, "oh God, Cathy we're really stuck. We have this diabetic kid who just came in service. We don't have a foster parent for them. They have no place to go. Can they stay with you?"

So we started doing what is called 'respite' which is basically an emergency placement or glorified babysitter for the medical kids. Finding foster homes is difficult enough, when you add a medical complication it becomes that much tougher because even if a person is willing they may not be qualified so they can't intake until they've had the medical training. Because I had the training and they knew me I was able to provide that temporary landing, the respite. And so through all of this process I got to see more and more into this world and I got to see more and more of what was happening.

But anyway one time I agreed to do respite for this diabetic little girl. She also had a brother so I just agreed to take both of them. It was supposed to be for a weekend to give their foster parents a break because she was a little bit of a handful. And so I went to pick these two kids.

When I got in the house the foster parents said, "we're not taking them back."

They never told the social worker anything. And all I can think at this point was, "oh my God, my husband is gonna kill me." So they packed up everything the kids had

entrepreneurs

in a trash bag and handed it to me without so much as a good luck. So here I am all their belongings in trash bags bringing it out to the car. All they can say is, "we don't want them back."

The kids are there in the room hearing this conversation. And, uhm, it really just, it really just affected me...

Carlos: That sounds heartbreaking.

Cathy Oskowiak: *It's terrible. It's really terrible. And this is just one of a gazillion stories like this. So again I'm diving deeper into this world, and becoming more emotionally entangled with everything, and learning more about the actual physical process of getting kids into homes, out of homes, and the entire functional side of the foster care system. So we were doing these respite cases and then they called me.*

"Cathy, we have this kid..." It's always 11:00 at night, raining, snowing, it's never convenient. "We're trying to locate the mom, but she's a runner. Would you be able to take them for the night? We don't have a place for them."

"Sure." And he came to the house. And when he came to the house he had nothing. He had: a onesie, a blanket, and the diaper he was wearing and that was it. And it was freezing out. And it's after midnight by this point and nothing is open. So first we prayed that he wouldn't wake up. Because he would be awake all night screaming. I mean think about it you wake up in a strange home with complete strangers. For an adult to process it would be terrifying. He was 13 months old. My second thought was, please don't soil your diaper. I don't have another one. The stores are closed. What am I going to do?

entrepreneurs

So that's kind of what sparked this idea. I started thinking these kids come with nothing. Or if it is anything it's literally a trash bag full of just stuff. Things that are often disgusting because they are usually unwashed which means they smells terrible. So I just learned so much more about the life of these kids and a lot of the time things are starting off horrible.

So all this is going on and I don't have a bottle for him. I don't have diapers for him. I don't have baby wipes or formula. I have nothing. So there was this panic and for the first time I was actually living it from the other end. Living this nightmare where all I wanted to do was help but had none of the tangible objects I needed to make it work. And I'm a trained pediatric nurse. It's my profession to care for children. I can't imagine how someone with limited resources or education would handle it. And so with all this; with my experiences as a nurse, with working so closely with the foster agency, we started up with this idea of doing backpacks. Providing backpacks for kids filled with basic care items.

Welfare gives foster kids backpacks. But they have a stigma attached to them. They're all the same so kids know what they look like especially the older kids. They're identifiable in schools as a welfare bag. Everybody knows they're welfare bags, kids, teachers, everyone and it can really make the kids feel ashamed, or embarrassed on top of the challenges of being a kid, and being a foster kid. And so talking with the adoption worker at the agency I'd been partnering with we kind of came up with the backpack idea. And that turned into us thinking well, we should really try to start this as an official 501(c)(3). Try to bring

entrepreneurs

attention to these issues so we can get help from corporate America and address these needs within the community. So our first step is educating the world about how the foster system works so we can find and partner with those people, those businesses that feel like they can help solve some of these very real problems.

And ultimately the end goal is to supply each child that goes into foster care a duffel bag of three days' worth of supplies that are age appropriate, and will work for everybody. And do so in real time. So they'll have what they need when they go into the foster home from the moment they step through that door. A baby will have diapers, bottles, formula, the basic needs will be meet if it's the middle of the night or there's a blizzard over the weekend and everything shuts down. It will be enough to get them through an emergent time until we can get them fully settled.

The other part to this is the foster parents do get a stipend, but often they won't get the stipend right away. They get it a month later, or at the month end. So they might not have the money in their budget to put out for the necessities. And from the kids' perspective to be able to be pulled out of probably one of the most horrific situations they've been in and placed into some stranger's house is traumatic. Especially the older kids who are able to remember. To be placed with some stranger you don't even know and then having to ask for deodorant or toothpaste is difficult. I just can't even imagine how much emotion is wrapped into something as simple brushing your teeth. There's embarrassment, or shame, or fear, or even confusion right? Not even understanding that it's okay to

entrepreneurs

ask for those things. That's normal, their situation is abnormal, but needing toothpaste is a normal thing. Asking someone for that is normal. But you're asking a stranger. And so it becomes wrapped in emotion. And a girl if she needs her own equipment depending what time of the month it is. I can't even imagine as a young girl asking a stranger for that.

So that's what we want to do. These bags will be designed to try to help give the kids some comfort. Give them three days' worth of clothes. Clean clothes. New clothes. Some of the kids have never had any new underwear or new anything in their life. And then also provide a comfort item, all their toiletries, a washcloth, a towel, just the basics. And so to give them new clothes and what they need it will allow them to go to school without that feeling of shame or embarrassment.

And hopefully during one of the most horrible parts of their lives, hopefully it'll give them just a little bit of comfort; just a small oasis of stability. Knowing that they have clean clothes, and a toothbrush, and the other small items its one less thing they have to worry about. And the idea is that it'll be a duffel bag that will be big enough to be a suitcase for them. Because most foster kids relocate between four and seven times before they either are adopted or age out of the system. And it is literally the standard practice that their stuff gets packed in trash bags. So an average of at least five times they're being told everything they own is garbage. That their lives are summed up into a big garbage bag, the thing we put on the curb for someone else to take away. Where's your dignity? How are you ever supposed to have self-esteem when everything you own is packed in a

entrepreneurs

trash bag? Your identity becomes tied to being trash. That you're trash...
Carlos: I feel sad now hearing this. I'm not gonna lie, I might start crying.
Cathy Oskowiak: *I'm trying not to cry too. I cry every time I talk about it, which won't be good if I ever need to speak about this with an executive board.*
Carlos: I think that's okay. I think it speaks to your passion. Not everyone, some people are just crybabies, but I think sometimes, maybe even a lot of times people who cry, they're not crying because of pain, and it's not because they're sad about something. They're crying because they feel so deeply and so passionate about whatever it is that is happening at that moment they cry.

And they can be angry, they can be disappointed, they can be excited, whatever that emotion is at that time, it's so overwhelming they just start crying. The emotion is so intense it overwhelms the rational portion of their brain. I'm starting to understand that that's okay. So if you start crying at the table, it's going in the book and it'll be all right. But I might join you. Just to give you a heads up.
Cathy Oskowiak: *Yeah. It's just, I just know what I live with, what I've experienced with my own son, and it's a lot for me to try and process. To feel like you don't belong and then to get a message that you're not anything. To be equated with trash because every piece of clothing you have is in a trash bag. And it's not everybody, but it's enough. It is more than I would ever wish. It's more than zero. And it's more than half of all foster kids. And so I just have this intense need to try to restore some dignity to*

entrepreneurs

these kids and try to make these kids fell like they are worth it. Like they're worth it; and they have meaning; and they have purpose; and they are somebody.

Carlos: It's tough enough, I think, teaching that to kids who aren't in the foster system. I can't imagine having to do that with kids in the system.

Cathy Oskowiak: *Right. We adopted my son at three and a half and he's gonna be 14 and we are still dealing with a lot of issues. And the on top of that he's a black kid in a white family and he has no freaking clue what his identity is.*

And there are times when he says he feels split. That part of him likes to be where he is, and loves his family, and loves his brothers and sister. And then part of him doesn't like to be where he is.

And I'll say, "well if you didn't want to be here, where would you be?"

"I want to live with a black family for two or three years and see how it goes."

And it's like, 'wow we're so easily dismissed.' But I had to get over my own self to understand that how confusing it must be. His entire journey so far. And he's 14 so at that age you're already going through a big transitional stage. And visually he can see that he's different. I think it would be a little bit different if it was just something that was internalized. If it was something that wasn't so visibly present. That visual cue does have an impact. And again, he's 14, so he's not emotionally mature enough to understand that you choose your identity. You can pick how you express the type of person you want to be. You literally choose who you are every single day. You

entrepreneurs

wake up and you can be whoever you want. And I would hope most people would choose to be someone good.

But we've been working like ten years on this, and one of the beautiful things about my husband and our relationship is that we are not afraid to change. To stop and think this parenting technique is not working. We're not stuck in the things we learned from our parents. We understand that what might have worked for one kid might not work for another, and we have reinvented our parenting a million times. Out of pure necessity we were forced to adapt. A big example is our standard practice was to put our bio kids in time out. And that worked. But try putting a kid in time out that never got any attention to begin with. Time out meant nothing. Time out was just business as usual, you know. We never parented a kid that when he did something wrong was already used to being ignored. The socialization growing up was different for him

Carlos: For all the talk about privilege, or advantage and all that stuff I think the biggest privilege that I ever had, the biggest advantage I ever had was I had two parents that loved me because more and more these days that experience is becoming rare a commodity. So the fact that he is in a loving home that is his advantage. The fact that you and your husband were able to give him that love is an amazingly powerful thing and I didn't understand that until recently. I think that really speaks a lot to who you are as a person. And I think that's really the key to giving him the tools that he needs. And with all that it sounds like it snowballed out of control and now you're here.

You mentioned before we started recording that you are not from the business world. You're a pediatric nurse.

entrepreneurs

You're starting this business. What were your first thoughts about that?

Cathy Oskowiak: *Adopting our son and becoming involved with the adoption agency is what triggered all of this. That passion became a hobby. First it was doing the charity, but it was through adopting our son that my eyes were opened to a whole world I knew nothing about. That passion is what drove me to turn this into a non-profit.*

On the other side of that, I was completely naive. The entire time I'm thinking yeah! Let's do this. We're gonna do this. We're gonna change the world. And in the beginning it was easy. Things kept falling into place but then you come up to a point where you run into your first barrier. For example, at first we funded the startup costs ourselves. We knew we needed some legal help establishing our business so we hired a lawyer. The lawyer came out of our pocket. And then other expenses were adding up. Nothing serious just little things, buying formula, buying bags, paying for different things was all self-funded in the beginning. But now it's at a point where that model isn't sustainable. We had stepped back and looked and realized okay, this is real and what do we do now? And how do we get where we want to be as soon as we can?

So I never looked at it like business. I looked at it more informally like, how do we grow this? How do we get this? How do we spread this? How do we make this national? How do we help these kids? There's half a million foster kids in the United States. How do we help these kids?

And maybe it was good that I never thought of it like a business, because if I had stopped and thought of it as a

entrepreneurs

business, I might not have ever really done it. I might not have taken that next step because thinking about that part -- I mean even right now as I'm talking to you -- that part seems really overwhelming to me. So I just have to keep talking myself through my own fears and remember why I'm doing it. Remember that we've gotten this far and things will happen and they'll happen when it's meant to happen.

Carlos: What I like about this, and again I think I told you earlier is that you're going through the startup process now. You're in it now. So it's gonna give a little bit different perspective than someone who's been in business five, ten, or even twenty years.

At each level you're gonna have something different. Everyone's gonna have a little bit different perspective. But let's say you're lucky and you make it to year ninety-nine, you're gonna know a lot more than someone who's in year one. But time heals all wounds, and as a result you might only remember the good experiences. People will tend to forget some of the less fun experiences they might have been going through at each step.

The other part to it is there is a theory about human behavior called an empathy gap. It basically states humans have a cognitive bias that causes people to underestimate how their current state of being influences their perception. Essentially the idea is that human understanding of a situation, or their perception, or their attitude towards something is extremely state dependent. So for example if you ask a business owner how the economy is doing and their business is doing great they might say the economy is great. But if sales were sluggish that day or that week they might give a different answer.

entrepreneurs

So I think having you give your perspective from that startup period. The perspective of being in the middle of launching your venture and going through all the struggles that a new business owner, a new entrepreneur, a new non-profit founder is going through is going to help. I think it's going to add value for someone who is thinking about starting their business or someone who is struggling during their own start up period. So that's why I'm excited about this. That's why I really like this. That's why I like getting your opinion. I think you can learn something from everyone.

Cathy Oskowiak: *Yeah. Yeah you have to be really open minded to be successful. And you have to keep your mind open to learn from each of your experiences. You mentioned that sometimes people can forget what it's like when you start out. And it's so funny that's one thing I actually always focused on and try to do. That's one thing that when I was going through the not so great things in my own life I really wanted to focus on. Remembering those feelings and what it felt like to struggle.*

When I was a brand-new nurse I was just overwhelmed with all the things I had to learn to do and it was exhausting and I was tired a lot and I was nervous because I didn't want to screw up. But I wanted to remember how that felt so I could help people going through that same experience when I became the teacher. Because of that, because I chose to do that, I can tell you today what it was like the day I gave my first shot. I honestly tried to never, ever forget that because it makes you a better teacher and it makes you a better person. And you can have the most knowledgeable nurse but if she forgets what

entrepreneurs

it's like to start out, then they lose something. They lose that empathy for someone who may be struggling at the start. And people don't get to benefit from that that great knowledge and experience.

Carlos: Yeah that's powerful. And I think it's important. And I think it's important in business as well just from a leadership perspective. Having the ability to relate to your team, or even more specifically, a new hire that maybe has the skillset but not the knowledge - if you're able to recognize where they might need support or help that empathy might be able to prevent a costly mistake.

But I'd like to pivot a bit here. You don't have a background in finance. You don't have a background in management. What do you think the biggest struggle so far has been in terms of getting this off the ground? Or maybe even just some of your fears, your concerns, you might have in moving this venture forward.

Cathy Oskowiak: *The biggest struggle to getting it off the ground really has been just finding the right people to financially invest in us. Finding the grants that are out there that are appropriate for us and match what it is we're trying to achieve. Because it's almost this is sort of catch-22 situation. Say you're applying for a grant or you want to talk to a corporate sponsor and they want to see how you've impacted the community. But I haven't had a huge chance to impact the community in the way that I would like because we're just starting out. With the charity I've certainly impacted the community in a positive way. We've helped thousands of kids but now we're expanding. And the type of changes that we want to make with the way we*

entrepreneurs

deliver help we just haven't even existed long enough to track that.

So you end up sort of in this catch-22 where you need to show results to seek investors but you need investors to get started to show results. It's almost like trying to find an angel investor, or get connected with somebody who will be willing to take a really big chance on you. So that's sort of where we're at right now. And you have people you're coming up against and competing with when it comes to grants, and they have been around for decades. We're coming up against people who have written grants for some really big non-profits. And here we are this little rinky-dink non-profit just starting out and trying to sort of compete without the knowledge base of finance, or grant writing, or interacting with corporate executives. So the knowledge base for me, the lack of knowledge in business, and finding those right connections is sort of the impasse that we're at now.

Carlos: Are you surprised how much of a business a non-profit actually functions as? Did it catch you off guard a little bit?

Cathy Oskowiak: *It's catching me off guard now. I'm such a passionate person that I let my passion run the whole thing to start. One thing I would say to people is that passion only takes you so far. And so now I'm at the point where I'm stepping back and going oh shit. Like what do I do? Am I biting off more than I can chew? We're just three people. We founded this with just three people. It's a social worker; my sister's in sales; and me, a nurse. I would never want to say I can't do something. I'll find a way. I will find a way to be successful at anything. I will fight tooth*

entrepreneurs

and nail to be successful but it's just trying to figure out where to go now. Like what the next step is it feels like we're spinning our wheels a bit.

Carlos: So that's one of the key characters of being the leader. You won't always have the answers but you'll ask the right questions and assemble the right team to help so you can do anything you set out to do. In terms of leadership, do you think that your experience as a pediatric nurse has helped you?

Cathy Oskowiak: *Leadership is probably the one thing I really feel confident about. And it's because I was a pediatric nurse I learned how, I mean really I had to learn how to communicate with people in a way that people can hear. You're dealing with people in a hospital, so already not at their best. The first half of that are the kids who are there for a reason. You're talking to them about medical stuff and you are explaining to a five-year-old about things adults might have trouble understanding. Second, because they are kids you automatically add a second patient and a third because the parents are involved. And now you're dealing with distraught parents. Their kids have cancer. How do you tell a parent that? How do you even explain cancer to a five-year-old, right? So I learned to communicate really well. And I think that is one of my better qualities; communication. And that has helped a ton.*

    Another piece to that is I always feel that everybody, everybody brings something to the table. It might not be that job that they're doing. Because quite honestly they might not be in that right job at the moment, but everybody has a purpose. And if you're a good leader, you just have to figure out what it is that people have and how you can

entrepreneurs

connect them with the right position so they can be productive. Because most people want to be, most people hate sitting around at work doing nothing. Everyone I know says the worst time at their job is when it's slow. When it's busy, they're not staring a clock, they're being productive.

So I have this vision. I know how I want this non-profit to go. I know how I want it to work and what I want it to accomplish. And I have the ability to communicate that vision and those goals to the right people; to our team so we can all work together to make sure it gets there. So I'm not fearful of being overwhelmed; that I'm not fearful of. I do get intimidated when I have to think about talking to people that are maybe on a higher education level than I am. Or I'm now entering the business world and I don't have that background. I do get intimidated when I'm trying to talk to people and not coming from that same background. Does that make sense? Like I'm confident in what I know but that drops off outside of that because I don't want to misrepresent myself or the non-profit.

The other part to leadership that I look at is like okay this problem came up. I can't solve it. Who can I reach out to? Because sometimes being a good leader isn't the fact that I have to know everything, it's that I have to know the people that know everything. And maybe that's what I need to do. Bring on the people that know more about the business side, know how to write the grants or know how to do this. I don't have to know it all. I just have to know who knows it. Or learn it.

I mean, what people can get done as a team versus what you can get done on your own, is just amazing and if you all pitch in for the greater good you'll be unstoppable.

entrepreneurs

My last job did not have any team work. It's like, everybody was out for themselves. My new job we all work together and it's amazing what you can get done when you all work together and you don't feel like you're alone.

And with the people that I'm working with now that's what it is. We're just all pitching in to get it done. And we do the jobs we don't like and we do the jobs we do like and we figure out who is better at talking to who. Now with the non-profit things are even bigger, and so that's what you have to do. There's no way you can know everything and if you try you're going to miss things. I'm not a lawyer so we hired one to make sure all our paperwork was done correctly. That's teamwork.

Carlos: You probably embody more leadership ability, and understand good leadership more than most of the managers I've ever met in my entire life. The fact that you're focused on communication; the fact that you understand that everyone is different and not just that but you have the ability to uniquely communicate with them; the fact that you understand that you can leverage human capital in a better way than maybe is better suited to them as a person and may not be related to their current job. You understand these concepts and not just understand them have implemented them. This is stuff I didn't understand or even know about until grad school. These are things you already know. You have the skills in place. You have the fundamental knowledge set to be successful. Not just in nursing, but as a business leader running a non-profit organization. Also I think you're saying some of the things that are common among entrepreneurs. And

entrepreneurs

you are an entrepreneur right now. I don't know if you view yourself that way.

Cathy Oskowiak: *Yeah. Hearing that, thinking about that sounds so bizarre to me actually. To think of myself as an entrepreneur. I've never thought about it that way. That's intimidating; that's a lot. I'll have to overcome my fear. I think that's... to be really honest I think deep down inside that's where I'm at with that. I sort of have this fear, some self-doubt about all of this. Every day I just keep waking up and I just have to force myself to try and not to think that way. Force myself to just focus and say okay, well I'm not gonna quit so what can I do next?*

Carlos: So you talked a little bit about your board members, you have two other board members. Can you talk about them? Who they are; how you met them?

Cathy Oskowiak: *So when we originally started out there were four of us. We had one person leave and their departure is definitely something I do feel bad about. But it's me, my sister, she's the one that's in sales. And then one of the social workers for the one agency we have mostly partnered with for the Christmas event, and who I worked with early on. And that's mostly because it's the agency we worked with when we adopted our son.*

We had another team member. Her husband was an entrepreneur. They stumbled on us last year doing another Christmas event which at that time it was me and my sister but they were interested in what we were doing and they asked if we were doing it all on our own. And at that point we were. It was my sister and me taking care of 450 kids and even more people dropping off gifts and you can't even imagine all the logistics involved.

entrepreneurs

Basically how the Christmas program works is this: We have the social workers at the agency ask the kids three things, three wishes for what they want for Christmas. Then my sister and I try to get people to adopt their wishes. And we usually ask for a minimum of $40 from each sponsor but there's no maximum. And we also ask that you try and get one out of the three wishes the child had within that $40 budget. So obviously you can't get them, I mean you can, but not like a car or anything just something you'd get for your niece or nephew.

And fortunately people have been extremely generous. People want to help. A lot of times they just need an idea. Sometimes people don't know what to do or how to help. So over the years people have just joined us and wanted to help in some way. And that's what happened with this couple. They kind of put the seed in our head. They recommended we make this official. And it was actually because of them that I just kind of said yeah, we can do this. Let's do this. And the husband had a little bit more knowledge and he had a little bit more experience from the business side.

So there were originally four but now the board is just the three of us, and then we have a board at large. So there are three voting members being my sister, our agency friend, and myself. The board at large is there for the functional aspects of things, support, growing ideas, providing expertise in different areas. So we have somebody who does marketing materials and stuff like that. She has been helping me out for years. We actually met in Girl Scouts and she's been helping me for years with the Christmas charity. She's super connected with the

entrepreneurs

community. She's a professor at Penn State and she's so connected in the higher education and she can get everybody involved with the gifts and everything. She's a great at developing resources. We have a designer, a graphic designer who also helps out with that.

And then we have another woman and she's plugged into the political world. She has political background with her family and she's a go getter. She's been great at generating contacts and different programs to look into. We also have somebody who has been on a non-profit board before to kind of help us along the way. And it's great to have their experience. That's most of the board at large. Those are the people we have and who we've been meeting with regularly as we move forward.

But now we're sort of at the step in the process where we need to expand the board and invite them to help regardless if they want to be voting members or not. Right now we are looking for people who can give more than just time. We really expand the board into connected people who share our passion and really want to take on more responsibility, and shoulder some of the burden, and help spread the word with their friends. Help us fundraise. Help us find the people who have the ability to become big sponsors. So we invited a child advocate attorney. He was actually my lawyer when we adopted our son. He's agreed to be on the board.

And we had a consultant come in and they were able to coach us a little bit and gave us some recommendations about how we can grow this because right now we're on a hamster wheel. We're just spinning around and we're not really propelling forward in the way I would like. So she

entrepreneurs

made us reevaluate our mission statement and our vision. We had to think about our strategy on how to implement our vision to accomplish our mission.

She came in and the first thing she asked was, "well, what do you want to be? Do you want to be a charity? Or do you want big time sponsorship? Or do you just want people to chip in and help? Do you want to ask a bunch of small businesses for a little bit of help? Or do you want to go for bigger corporate sponsors? If you want to go for big corporate sponsors you need to give them something. So what are you gonna give them?"

I didn't even really know that there was a huge difference in that world. We decided we need to start with education. Educate them on what it's like out there. As a result, we made a sort of change to our mission statement. We changed our mission statement to reflect the fact that we want to educate people about the foster care system in America. And we want to try and even out the playing field with the kids in the care versus kids not in care. So she's been able to get us to look at our approach a little bit differently and understand that this is a business. Our marketing to small, individual donors is going to be different than going after large corporate sponsors because each of those groups is going to want something different in return.

But we're in the thick of the Christmas event right now so we don't have a rigid schedule to meet right now because it's really just a full time job for all of us. So starting January we're gonna be bringing some more members in. Anybody who might be interested in what we are doing. Anyone that can help us; that can help us

entrepreneurs

financially; can help us during tax time with filing; help us with knowledge; help us make the right kind of connections. That's where we're at. Not that easy.

Carlos: So let me kind of rewind a little bit. Am I correct in understanding that it was you and your sister managing the logistics for roughly 450 children? And for each of those children you were tracking a wish list of three gifts, and then managing 450 sponsors on top of that. So basically you were providing the logistics for and connecting almost 1000 people during Christmas time. Christmas time which is a time that is notoriously hectic; it is notoriously stressful; it is a season when most people have their own families to take care of from big meal planning, to holiday parties, and gift giving, all of those things. Would that be an accurate description of what I'm hearing? Because that sounds to me a lot like you were an operations manager. So you've spent the past ten years as an operations manager. You have the chops for running a business because you basically, functionally you ran a business. Not only did you run a business, you grew a business 9 fold in ten years.

You opened this conversation up with, "I don't know what I'm doing. I'm not in business."

You've been running a business for ten years. But the reason I bring this up and I think what is important for people to understand, and hopefully who somebody reads this that feels this way will understand, I think a lot of times we get down on ourselves. Not like we're feeling sorry for ourselves, or moping about, or anything like that but we underestimate our own ability. And we can't see the forest through the trees, I think a little bit.

entrepreneurs

Because I've been sitting here listening to you, processing what you're saying and the more you say, and the more I understand, it has been this slow realization washing over me. I literally found myself thinking you've been running a business for ten years now. You just haven't looked at it that way. And I think it's because you've been so passionate about it and because you've been so focused on your mission. And I think a lot of young entrepreneurs might feel the same way.

It's the mindset of: I'm not running a business I'm just baking cupcakes. I just really like making cupcakes and I am really good at it, I make them for all my friends and family, and I sell them at the farmer's market on Sunday because it gets me out of the house. And people don't stop to think that functionally they're operating a business. That is a business. Some of your customers didn't pay. You're giving away product and that's called marketing. But one of the most fundamental forms of business is making a product and getting customers. I think a lot of people miss that sometimes.

But if you've been doing that, and it's been successful, I think you should take at least a little bit of credit for that. You should take some recognition which is weird for a lot of people and that's one of the other common things that I've noticed about entrepreneurs. Real successful people never really feel like they're successful yet. Or it took a long time for them to accept that about themselves. It's that missing piece that keeps them driving up the mountain. Like they can never reach the top so they keep climbing. But I think that mentality is

entrepreneurs

what separates somebody from being complacent to being successful.

So, I just wanted to give you some of that feedback right now because I think it's important. You've literally been talking about everything that I had to learn in business school. You've been talking about it, you've been doing it. Understanding when you make mistakes, communicating, understanding the value of teamwork, understanding the value people, operations management, all the things you talked about are the keys to running a successful business. You have those abilities already. You have the tools that you are gonna need to be successful with this.

Cathy Oskowiak: *Thanks. It actually, I seriously, never even thought about it like that. And when you put it that way it doesn't sound bad. I think just like you were saying I always thought just, oh yay, you went from 50 to 450 kids. No big deal, we could have done more. And yeah just figuring out a way to make things work. We never said no to anybody. We will not say no. If we have all the kids covered, we'll find another one to cover. And that drive it comes from my family. And not accepting anything less than being successful. That's all.*

Carlos: What has been your biggest success so far in terms of either the Christmas event or in the first ten months for Foster Angels?

Cathy Oskowiak: *The biggest moment for me is when we managed to get three bags out to kids in real time. There was a sibling group going out into foster care. They were going into a family placement. A family placement is when kids are being moved in with an existing relative. In*

entrepreneurs

this case it was the grandmother and she had nothing. There was an aunt or another family member living there as well helping but they were an adult. But the household wasn't prepared for three children. It actually felt really good to get those three bags out. Aside from the Christmas event we also do a spring fling type party for a group of kids, and then we also have a backpack program that we did for about 400 kids previously. But this was the first time it was in real time as the kids transitioned out of their home into foster care. It's only been those three bags so far but it's the first time that we got to do what we wanted to do. What we set out to do. And it worked. It was definitely proof of concept.

    As far as when I'll be successful, or when we will be successful? I want to be successful tomorrow. I want to be an international name tomorrow. I have to stop myself and remember we didn't go from 50 to 450 overnight. There's a process. Growth takes time and it's a process. It takes patience and hard work and sometimes you just have to be patient and keep moving along. So that's what I'm trying to do. And in the meantime be a magnet to other people who believe in our mission and want to see it move forward.

    But getting those bags out and seeing that it worked, and seeing the impact definitely energized me. I have this picture. This vision in my head and seeing it happen with those first three was big. It just made me feel really good. But we have been self-funding so far. Not the Christmas portion but like getting the lawyer and setting everything up, and those three bags were all from us. And the sad thing is that right now I just don't have the funds to keep doing that. And that's part of why we wanted to make this

entrepreneurs

a real non-profit. But those three, seeing it work, that felt really good. And it really helped the foster parents. It helped the kids. And it helped fuel what we do. So that's been the biggest thing. That was my biggest moment.
Carlos: Moving forward, what do you think your biggest challenge is going to be?
Cathy Oskowiak: *Moving forward, the biggest challenge is going to be getting the right people on our board. Finding the right people who are willing to commit to even half of what we do. People who are committed to really help drive this forward are tough to find. That is the biggest challenge we have right now. I think you talked about it finding the right employees that are a good fit for your culture.*

That and then what does forward look like? I know the end result. I know how I want to implement. I know we need revenue. But how do we do it right? What's gonna be next? You know. There some things like, hey if we want to take this national, there's a huge diversity across the country. There are variations as to why kids are going into care. In one state it might be primarily due to drug use or in another it might be single parenthood, or economic burden. Each state is different than the next.

So we need like a diverse group of people to understand the needs for each area. We need the lawyers who know the law for each state. New York might have different rules for how we interact with the kids because they are kids. We need people in finance, people to help us maximize how we're using our funding. We need people that can speak different languages. There are a lot of Spanish speaking kids, and foster parents. Not everybody speaks English, even on the volunteer side. There are

entrepreneurs

people who want to help but maybe we're not reaching or we can't hear their voice because we don't have someone who can do outreach in Spanish. But if we have one person who can speak the language of whoever we're trying to target or join or help it could make the difference. Diversity is the key. It's everything.

Carlos: Did you ever want to quit while you were going through this process?

Cathy Oskowiak: *Yeah. The day I ran into you. And there have been a few times that I have struggled. There were a couple times when it was still just the Christmas Angels I wanted to quit. Before this even became a non-profit because for seven out of those ten years prior to becoming a non-profit, I did it myself. I didn't have the committed help that I have now. So there were a lot of times along the way because and we already talked about but it is enormously time consuming. I have five kids, five active young kids. I have Christmas to do for five kids. I was Girl Scout leader. I was not only a Girl Scout leader but I was the leader for two troops. So that's 25 in each troop. I had 50 kids all together just for girl scouts. On top of that I was also the Service Unit manager and the cookie manager.*

So, I was doing a lot. Part of that and something that is a whole other story aside is that was my escape from dealing with ugliness in my life. I was committing myself to everybody else to avoid those things. But yeah a couple times I did wanna quit. And I was serious about it. I talked to my husband about it and was just to the point where I just felt like I can't do this anymore. And my husband was very supportive and he knew I wanted to quit but he was able to help me find my way. And he did so by just helping.

entrepreneurs

He would say, "these are the kids. You love them. You know you gotta do this."

So whenever I felt like that, whenever I would feel like quitting he supported me. And my husband was the one person I was the most honest with about it. Every time I told him I don't know if I can do this anymore he would just look at me and tell me I could give up something else. He knew I would regret giving up on the kids. And so he was always, always there. Not pushing me along, not dragging me, but more of just holding my hand and providing stability for me.

You know I believe in divine intervention and there have been couple times it's happened. The day I met you in the store is one of them. I think I told you I was very seriously considering just giving up on the non-profit portion. I was at the point where I was extremely overwhelmed. I had a lot going on with my own kids. In the past two and a half years I've had a person close to me attempt suicide and then literally two years after that I was going through the same thing with another person. And between all the doctor appointments they also have band or soccer or school work. And then my other son he has his own issues from foster care.

So, I had a lot going on. My full time job has been keeping me very busy this year. So my professional work has taken a lot more. For most of those years I was an at home mom and things were much easier to manage. But we were just getting to the point where, we were just thinking about how we need to grow it. I was becoming seriously overwhelmed by everything. I was thinking that I should just scale it back to just the Christmas event. I was just at

entrepreneurs

the point where I didn't know if I could do this anymore. I just didn't know if I had the capacity to keep moving. My head was barely afloat and the fact that this wasn't going as easy as when it started to go at first and all these roadblocks and struggles cropped up all at once.

And then I ran into you. And I just believe any time I've ever been at a crossroads with life I've been divinely shown the way I need to go and that if I'm open to listening to the cues then I'll be able to hear and see the way. And my husband has been supportive as always constantly cheering me on, telling me I can't give this up. He knows I need to do this. So three weeks ago I was ready to quit. Yeah.

Carlos: That's amazing. And now I hear you talking and it sounds like you're more passionate than ever.

Cathy Oskowiak: *Yeah. Yeah I am because the Christmas thing really helps refuel me again. Part of that is that it's just one agency that we're dealing with and we have over 400 children again. Before Christmas arrives there's gonna be more kids in care. One every three minutes in America. So one agency out of hundreds has over 400 kids. That shows me there are kids that are out there in need.*

The other half of that is all the support we get for it. That alone shows me how committed people are to helping. It shows me the goodness of the world. People really do want to help. They just need to know how to help, or where to help. And so it kind of, it definitely propels me.

Carlos: That's awesome. That's really great that the community is so supportive. That they're able to provide that for the kids and participate at such a direct level is amazing.

entrepreneurs

For the non-profit side, it is a business structure but it's a bit different. For example, do you have direct reports? You are the organizational leader, so it's more egalitarian than hierarchical I would imagine. Everyone is more on equal footing in terms of individual decision making. And you're small enough that organizational size isn't really driving the need for bureaucracy to provide organization and stability.

And even though you are the head of the board people can just walk away. Their income isn't tied to their performance within your organization. The power dynamic changes when people don't have the same concerns a typical employee might have. How do you approach that when issues arise?

Cathy Oskowiak: *So for the first part of that, the three of us each have what we're good at and then the people that are under us, or working directly with us help us within each of those areas. I have a friend who helps who has a very high level professional job at Aramark. She's very successful there, and because of her experience she's been really good at helping develop budgets, and some of the finance and operations. That was even overwhelming on the application because how do you budget something when you have no money? Or project a budget? I never projected a budget before. But she was able to really help me with that.*

So we do have kind of direct reports. Our social worker partner is in charge of the community outreach and programing. She has two people that work with her. I have two people I work with that help me. They're sort of like my business development advisors. They have more experience

entrepreneurs

with that. And then my sister works directly with the marketing person; develop marketing materials and things like that. So in a very small scale we have what could be called division meetings. Because we don't all need to meet about the same thing, you know.

But again the biggest challenge is: they're not making any money from this business. So how do you keep people invested? How do you how do we provide value for them? That's the thing that will keep them coming back. If they believe in the mission, if they can understand the vision, and they feel like they're helping to achieve those things. Because we're not giving them an income and I certainly learned from our fourth board member what it felt like to lose someone. And I don't want that to happen again so how do we keep people invested, engaged, and help them feel like they're important? Like the work they're doing is important. I think just making them feel appreciated and valued goes a long way.

Carlos: *There is definitely a different dynamic. What do you think the most difficult part about managing personalities and relationships is?*

Cathy Oskowiak: *So, I enjoy the challenge of trying to figure out how to connect with each person. I believe that every single one of us in the world is connected somehow. I view it like it's my job to figure out how we are connected. And once you connect with people, once you find out how you're connected, then you build it on that connection. You strengthen it. I try to make every person I ever meet, and not to over simplify it but I try to make every person I ever meet a friend, because you treat your friends better than you treat a stranger.*

entrepreneurs

So I try to take that experience I learned in nursing, and how I approach things in life, I try and take that with me in what I'm doing with Foster Angels. I try to find that one thing that I'm connected to other people with and I try to then expand on it and grow it. Then you gain their trust, then you gain their understanding. And if I'm open to listen to people, then I can hear what's important to them and figure out the best place for them. Did that answer it? Or did I go off on a tangent?

Carlos: No that's great. I love your answers so far. So, what have you liked the most about this experience so far?

Cathy Oskowiak: *There are so many things. The biggest thing is knowing that we can make one kid's life a smidge better. And I'm not so naïve to say a bag is gonna make them the happiest kid in the world. It's not going to solve all their problems. But if I can make their life a smidge better and just be one little piece of glitter for them, it can open a world to more. It might show them there are good things out there and there are good people out there.*

Or knowing that a Christmas presents gives one kid a smile; I'll never have to see it. I have seen it because we use to do a big luncheon for them when it was smaller. So I saw how they reacted and I keep that with me in my heart. But knowing that you have the ability to possibly change somebody's life for better is the most amazing feeling. All this, doing all of the work with Christmas angels, and teaching, and all of it also brought me on a spiritual journey. And then working with some really amazing people and who are just as committed. Seeing their commitment, seeing that they won't give up either, and it's hard for all of us we all have jobs and kids but seeing that in another

entrepreneurs

person and knowing there's more people like that. That's been amazing. And so there's so many things that I have gotten from and continue to get every day there isn't just one. Because in every aspect of it there been something amazing I've been able to experience.

Carlos: So being that you're a non-profit, your return on investment is seeing those improved outcomes within the community. In a for-profit business the return on investment is monetary. The goal is to secure market segments to capture those revenue dollars and generate profit. It's a competition. There's also competition in the non-profit sector. We talked a little bit about competing for grants. For example, most companies only budget X amount of dollars to donate and once the budget is consumed they can't give anymore.

Knowing that you're competing against people in a similar space who also are trying to accomplish some of the same goals as you how do you process that? Do you process that?

Cathy Oskowiak: *Yeah at the end of the day, they all go to something wonderful. So that's a win for everybody. But I told you earlier I like a challenge. I love a challenge. And I hate to admit it but I'm super competitive. I'm a little more chill about it but I'm really competitive. So I'm not going to get the grants at first. I don't know the language. I don't have the experience. I'm not an established non-profit. But that's learning. Going through all of these struggles and thinking okay, why did I lose that one? How could I do it different next time?*

And knowing my market. I still have to know my market. I have to know what's out there. There are

entrepreneurs

organizations and other non-profits in the same space. There are people that are doing something similar with bags. I'd be foolish to say we're the only ones. We're not. But not many that I know of are doing it in real time. Now I've just differentiated. How else can we be different? How can we stand out and make ourselves noticed? How can I do it better? So it's learning what your competitor does and figuring out how you do it better. And so I've turned it into a problem solving challenge. And I love solving problems.

For more information about Foster Angles on Earth go to: www.FosterAngelsOnEarth.com

take away

So how can this help you? Well you might be thinking you don't have the skills or tacit knowledge capable of running your own business. I never thought I could own my own company or write my own corporate charter. I don't know very much about accounting. And if you're reading this because you are considering starting your own company one day you might be thinking to yourself, "I have no clue how to file quarterly taxes." But after speaking with Cathy I don't believe knowing all of those mechanical functions for operating a business are a prerequisite for chasing your dreams. Will those skills help? Certainly. Should not knowing them stop you? I would argue no, and Cathy helped me to see that. Even though I might not know how to develop a corporate charter or track revenue for accounting purposes, there

entrepreneurs

are very talented people who do. I can and should seek them out to ask for their help.

This realization also helped me to understand that great leaders don't know how to do everything. One common trait I've witnessed repeatedly among experienced and effective leaders is a humble self awareness. They acknowledge their own weaknesses and then find team members who can fill those gaps. When Cathy decided to launch her nonprofit group she didn't know everything about running a business. She wasn't an accountant, or finance major. She had never started a company or written a corporate charter. So she found people who could, and asked for their help. She acknowledged the gaps in her own experience and sought out others who did have those value added skills to launch a business.

Finding a group of people who compliment one another's strengths and cover their weaknesses can prove to be the critical factor for a high performance team. Not only does it help prevent blind spots when addressing problems that may arise, but more importantly: it builds trust. Developing and fostering an environment of trust is foundational to establishing a healthy work culture, and an effective strategy to driving engagement in the workplace.

We all rely on and trust and trust people in our lives. This trust can take the mundane form of trusting that other drivers won't swerve into us on the highway; to more complex trust that our accountant will file our taxes on time; to the impossible complexities of love and trusting our romantic partners. While we may not actively think to ourselves how grateful we are the server who

entrepreneurs

brought our food didn't poison it; we often explicitly think about whether or not our co-workers are trustworthy. And the less energy we spend on worrying about trust, the more energy we have for other tasks.

Another reason I believe Cathy is a great example of a strong and effective leader is that she clearly established why her non-profit should exist.[4] If you know why your business will exist and then surround yourself with people who feel the same you're building in team engagement. Cathy knows the why for her venture: help foster children. She has established the purpose of her business. She was able to identify people who also believed in what she was doing and they each brought their skills, strengths, and ideas. And together they worked to build their venture into a success.

Once you're able to define that why, it becomes much easier to find people who are similarly passionate and believe in doing the same. Not because those people will stand out like a beacon of light, but because you'll be able to narrow your field of choices. You can intentionally seek out other individuals that believe helping foster children is a noble reason for a business to exist. From there you can assemble a team centered around that why. That team will have built in motivation and will support the mission from day one. And those team members you find aren't just warm bodies. You can target specific people who bring with them skills and experience your team will need to develop and grow your business.

---

[4] This "why" is much talked about by Simon Sinek in his book, _Start With Why_ which I highly recommend reading.

entrepreneurs

So Cathy found people who: a) believed in the why b) added skills to the team. Cathy put her trust in people she had to rely on for skills she didn't possess, and when they demonstrated competency in their role her trust was confirmed. In turn they reciprocated that trust in Cathy and teamwork increased. As she showed she appreciated and valued their work they reciprocated and became even more passionate about what they were doing. This is how you can drive success not only in starting a business but also in being a good leader. You don't need to know everything about accounting; just find a good accountant you can trust.

A year out from the interview I thought about what I had learned from Cathy's story and what had really stuck with me. Then I thought back to what had initially grabbed me and made me interested in interviewing her as a part of this project. I think it was how very exposed she was. This is a similar sentiment that I sensed during all of my interviews but it was more intense with Cathy. She has an extremely personal interest in seeing her venture succeed outside of the mission statement. This wasn't about providing for her family, personal enrichment, or self glorification. I think if we examined decisions that people made, and put them on a spectrum at one end would be purely selfless acts, and opposite that were purely selfish acts Cathy's story would be closer to the selfless end. She wants to succeed because of a selfless drive and determination to help others. There is also an emotional tie directly linked to her love for her family. It's that love that fuels her passion for her project, and drives her decision making. And while not every decision will be

entrepreneurs

the right decision they will be made in good faith towards achieving the mission.

That level of passion and excitement won't be a part of most people's entrepreneurial ventures. I don't think it's reasonable, or even necessary to project that level of expectation onto anyone. We all have bills to pay, and family's to care for. But that's what makes Cathy's story so unique. During the interview she had shared with me an experience that is special: it is both inspirational and aspirational. I look at her determination, passion, and selflessness and I can use her experiences to help make better decisions while I am navigating through my daily struggles. I can be more effective at my job. I can stay just a little bit later to help my team. I can exercise more patience and understanding when I get frustrated. I can be just a little more humble.

Why I think it's useful to discuss and consider the ideas Cathy's interview presented is that I do fully believe passion has to be at least a small part of any entrepreneur's motivation. Without at least some passion I would argue it's far easier to simply get a job working for someone else. Some people might say, "well I don't want easy, that's why I own my own business." It's exactly that sentiment I believe to be the passion to live your best life. Driven to face unknown challenges of the world. It's a passion focused on the outcome or the experience rather than the modality. Some people might enjoy the freedom being your own boss provides, or the knowledge they are making their own way with no safety net. These are examples of how a passion for something can be the driving motivation to open a cafe, or start a new marketing

entrepreneurs

company. The passion might not be specific to serving coffee or selling marketing experiences to clients, but the fulfilment in doing those things as an entrepreneur provides. It can be the fuel for your drive to succeed.

entrepreneurs

Charlie Collazo: The Institute

Charlie Collazo is a serial entrepreneur. He's opened multiple businesses. He's seen both success and failure. He grew up in Philadelphia, and has witnessed the city undergo a number of changes over the years. He's seen the skyline transform, and feels the new energy and vibrancy growing in the city. And while he enjoys the new life, people, and opportunity Philadelphia's rebirth has brought he also reminisces about losing the Philly of his childhood; a rough and gritty town filled with generational corner stores, and bodega cats.

Charlie is a family man. He has five children. He loves them, and works ridiculously hard to support them. I've known Charlie Collazo for just over 5 years now. The Institute was the second bar I tried when I moved to Philly, and I have spent a lot of time there. Charlie is one of those people who will never stop working. If he won the lottery tomorrow, he would still be out there hammering away chasing success, continuing to build, continuing to create, and continuing to hustle. He might take a few months off, but he would end up back in the mix, creating and building his next venture.

I feel extremely fortunate that he was willing to share some of his experiences with me. I hope you can recognize the same passion, and humanity that I see in Charlie, and I hope you enjoy learning from his experiences as much as I did.

entrepreneurs

ф

Carlos: We're recording. I have a few questions laid out but I figured we could just see how things go. Let's start with something easy, your name?

Charlie Collazo: *Carlos Collazo Jr.*

Carlos: But everyone knows you as Charlie? Was that something you picked or was it just kind of assigned?

Charlie Collazo: *It was a little of both. Since I'm a junior my mom needed to us to know which Carlos was the one she was cursing out in Spanish. (laughs)*

Carlos: That's too funny. And you own The Institute, which is a corner bar in Philadelphia. How long have you been operating?

Charlie Collazo: *Nine years. We opened in June 2008.*

Carlos: And how did you get started in this industry? Did you always want to open a bar?

Charlie Collazo: *I was actually an operations manager for Home Depot. But I had a family, and bills, and a mortgage, so I had a side hustle too. I had started doing part-time work on the weekends installing and programming lighting systems for nightclubs. And because I knew how to do the installs, it turned into a second side job operating the systems on the weekends for the owners.*

At the time, we had just finished renovating our house, which was also in the neighborhood, and we were looking to pull out equity out of the house and possibly invest in some other real estate, or possibly a corner property with a corner store. We had seen the bar for sale, which is what got us thinking about doing this type of investment. Once we started looking, we had actually forgotten that the bar was for sale. After looking around at

entrepreneurs

different properties in different areas, we saw the bar was still up for sale so we took a look at it. I talked to my wife and after about 30 minutes we decided we were gonna go all in on buying the bar.

We looked the market in the city, and we decided we were going to change it into a craft-beer bar. Things in the city were changing really quickly. New kids were moving into the neighborhood, Temple was growing, and gastropubs were becoming very popular. With that came a lot of different craft breweries. The local beer like Yards was grown; Philadelphia Brewing Company started the year before maybe, and an older brand like Yuengling, because it was local, was big in the city. And there were other more national brands as well we wanted to bring in.

Carlos: So, you opened in 2008. That was an interesting year. The Phillies won the series. But that was also the year the recession hit. Your first year open, and the economy tanks how did you survive through that?

Charlie Collazo: *That's the interesting thing because recessions typically are one of those things that don't have as big an impact on places like bars. People want to drink either to celebrate the good times, or forget the bad. But it does have a much larger impact on places that are more of a restaurant establishment. People will skip going out for dinner, eat at home, and then stop in and drink a beer, or get take out (beer). We are known more as a beer establishment and the corner bar.*

That's usually what happens when times are tight and people are out of work and stuff. They're not going out and spending money on meals. So if you're not going out for dinner where you'll usually get a drink, but you still want

entrepreneurs

to get a drink, you'll go to the beer distributor, or the nearest take out place. So we pretty much kept going right through with no real issues at the time. It might have actually brought us customers who normally would have passed over us for a sit down restaurant.

Carlos: What is your favorite thing about owning your own business?

Charlie Collazo: *Not having to answer to anyone else, with the exception of the city, state, and federal revenue departments. (laughs) But seriously, I really love the freedom of being my own boss. I know that my success is based on how hard I want to work. How much effort I'm willing to put into making this place successful.*

A lot of people will say like, "oh but what if the economy gets bad" or whatever.

But that can happen when you're working any job. Look at all the people who lost their jobs and everything in 2008. They were working in finance, they working at banks. What was that movie? They were too big to fail? Yeah, and they failed. And nobody thought it could happen. These jobs were the safe jobs.

Carlos: What worries you the most about your business?

Charlie Collazo: *Having to answer to the city, state and federal agencies (laughs). With just a quick waving of a pen and a signature they can shut you down. Depending on what the issue might be, and there's no recourse. They don't look at what that really means for a small business owner. How much you've risked. How much you have riding on whether or not you're open for that day, or that weekend. If we get shut down on a Friday, that probably means we're shut down for the weekend, and those are the*

entrepreneurs

days we make money to float us through the week. So when they talk about coming in because let's say you have a tax issue. And maybe it's that you're just backed up on taxes.

Or maybe a better example is if licensing and inspection comes in and they tell you, "Oh, well you have this wrong and we're going to close your entire business down."

Look, I get it when it comes to things like public safety, or there's a health issue at stake. I do understand. People's lives can be put in jeopardy with some things. And every business owner has the responsibility to make certain they are conducting their business properly and safely. That's one thing. But when one bad inspector can continuously hammer you for small, petty little things it becomes extremely frustrating. The sense of fair play is diminished by one person.

For example the recommendations for a fire nozzle changed one year to the next and this inspector doesn't know if you have the old style you can keep it but instead they shut you down. Now you have to go to the city and show your permits from when the work was done but you're not allowed to use your fryer all weekend and that's a huge part of sales. Or worse they completely close you and you're out 10 thousand dollars. Now your employees can't come to work. Or they're going to make a lot less money, and now they're behind on their bills. All of those people are screwed because of one incorrect code reading. That's pretty scary and can be intimidating especially for a new business owner. And I think what drives that feeling of frustration more than anything is the lack of consistency

entrepreneurs

from one inspector to the next. And to be fair to the inspectors they have a tough job. City codes can change year to year, and for some of them it's only a part time job.
Carlos: That's, yeah that's scary. I don't think very many people think of those types of things when they're advocating for more business regulations. I think people believe it's all upside. That if businesses are fighting it then it must be good for the public and what they don't hear, or maybe don't want to believe is that there can be a downside as well and as a society we should really examine what the tradeoffs will be, and are we okay with that. And maybe we are okay with it, but we need to have those discussions. It's probably somewhere in the middle.

Moving on, let's pivot to something a bit more upbeat. What's been your biggest success so far?
Charlie Collazo: *That's hard to say. I don't really think I can measure my success yet. Like I don't think I'm successful yet. Partially because I'm not in the position where I can say I'm going to take a vacation for like two or three weeks. So I kind of feel like I'm not quite there yet when I think of what success looks like. I mean I still have that drive to work harder than the average person. I do work harder that the average person because the average person has their 40 to 50-hour week. That's it. They go home, and they've got their weekends, or at least two days off.*

For me it feels great to own a business. I have a lot of freedom. But if I want to eventually become successful, it means I have to put the work in. It means I'm on call seven days a week. I'm constantly fixing problems, handling the different things that inevitably crop up during the week. So

entrepreneurs

until I can have a vacation, or I can have normal days off, or I can relax a little, which I am always moving, always going, I won't feel like I've hit success. Not yet anyway. I measure success on a different scale. I think success is a level of comfort in life. I don't need riches, money, fancy cars, and all that stuff. Just being able to just actually have normal days off is when I'll know. Kind of have some normalcy to my hours. When I get to that point that's how I'll know. That's how I kind of gauge my success.

Carlos: That's interesting. You've been successfully operating this business for nine years, and you still don't feel like that's success. And you've survived longer than the average business, not just survived but thrived and used your success here to map out other ventures. What would you say in the first nine years has been your biggest failure?

Charlie Collazo: *I've had a few failures. I've tried a few different things that didn't really work out. I tried a coffee shop and tattoo studio. That didn't work out. I tried doing a kitchen at another nightclub establishment. That didn't work out. Just recently opened up a new place and I don't know if I can necessarily say it's a failure because like any new business it takes some time to establish particularly for a neighborhood bar like that. But I didn't get a chance to really make it succeed because I've decided to sell it in anticipation of doing something bigger with The Institute.*

  So even though I didn't get it really an opportunity to make it flourish and succeed, I kind of feel like it's a failure because selling it and getting rid of it. But I was still in the process of trying to make it succeed. So it's sort of, it just

entrepreneurs

feels like a failure to me. Like I didn't achieve what all I could achieve with it.

But with all of those attempts, all of those ventures, I learned something new like some new experience or new way to go around certain barriers. I learned something that has made the bar better, or made me better at doing new things. So it's like I'm getting better at all thing things I'm doing and it'll all add up.

Carlos: So you currently own two bars, the Institute and a second bar in South Philly and you've actually decided to sell the place in South Philly. Was that decision based on finance?

Charlie Collazo: *Yeah, I'm freeing up some working capital. With any new establishment it takes you a year or two years to establish that place to the point where it's financially independent and stable. Right now, it's not financially independent and I am leveraging bank financing to keep that afloat and pay the bills while it develops. With the move that I'm making with The Institute to its new location, I have to choose. I won't be able to do both businesses because it'll overextend my credit with the bank.*

That's why I have to let things stay status quo with The Institute, leverage what I'm doing here to launch the new location which will be a much better space for the business, for the employees, and for the customers. So it's kind of an easy decision, even though it means giving up another project. Almost like a stereotypical business case. Do I make investment A or go with project B? And looking at everything, this was the right decision for me and the business.

entrepreneurs

Carlos: With the other bar it's more of a strategic decision than a failure. It didn't fail financially, you're just in a position to make a different investment with your money and you have to decide which has the better upside.

Charlie Collazo: *Yeah, you can say it's a strategic decision. I just, in my mind, I just feel like it's a failure though. That's just me.*

Carlos: Do you think that's part of what made you successful? Almost like things are never good enough.

Charlie Collazo: *I think so. I think it's like I said before about success. That even though I have the bar I don't feel like I can say that I'm this big success. Like I can't measure the things I've done and see them or see myself as being successful. I think that's what it is that drives me to achieve. That constant carrot of success I keep chasing. That's definitely part of it.*

The other thing would be my children. That's probably the biggest part of why I'm so driven because at the end of the day I have a family. I have kids. I can't stick my tail between my legs and then put my head in a hole, and be like, "oh, this didn't work and boohoo for me." Well, okay that's shitty that things didn't work. What am I gonna do next? Because I've got kids to feed and I have to keep a roof over their head. So I think my kids are really my biggest like driving factor in that thing that keeps me going every day. It definitely makes me put in the insane hours.

Carlos: Yeah, you do work crazy hours. I know. I have been here drinking for a lot of them. What gets you most excited about owning your own business?

Charlie Collazo: *There are a few different things. My real passion is the designing and the building. The hands on*

entrepreneurs

stuff, that's what gets me really excited. When I get to lay out new designs, and different ideas, and then actually execute and build them myself.

A lot of it is the customers as well. That part of the business also gets me excited. Probably more so than the building I think because interacting with customers and talking to people, it's just a great feeling when you have people who will talk with you, and they'll share their lives with you.

And then they tell you like, "oh I know that place. Dude, that's really cool. I've been there before and I like your place. You guys are doing a good job."

It's always a good feeling when people tell you that they like your establishment. That the space you've built can give people a good feeling and they feel comfortable sharing that with you, and with their friends and stuff. And I always enjoy just interacting with customers in general. You get the chance to meet so many interesting people in the business.

Unfortunately, over the past few years for me it's gotten a little hard because I work so much. You get to those points later in each day, and then into the evenings, and you really don't wanna engage as much. So you sacrifice that conversation with customers because you've been going at it all day. But it's hard because it's your job to give good customer service. It's part of the business and that's what people enjoy. People enjoy meeting the owners of places and stuff, and having conversations, and asking questions, and they feel connected. And they are. I know all my regulars and I invite them out, and I'll put together events for the people I see regularly. And those are the

entrepreneurs

things that people remember and helps draw customers back to a place. When they have that positive interaction with an owner and stuff, most people will feel more connected when they see the owner.

They say, "Oh wow! That's the owner."

And then on top of it they're like, "Yeah that owner is in the trenches, he's in there working. He's busting ass."

They know, and they see that it's not just some guy just sitting home, coming in and collecting money. It creates another level of respect from customers. That's the best feeling in the world. And it's pretty cool for me to feel that from customers. Building a human connection with them is really, really fun.

Carlos: I imagine that it's not all roses and sunshine. I think it's Tim Ferris that says, or believes in, firing your worst customers. That 20% of your customers dominate 80% of your time, and that you should find ways to get rid of that 20%. What would you say the biggest challenge from the customers is?

Charlie Collazo: *Trying to keep pace with things as they change. The demand of what customers want to see on the menu, or on the draft list. It's very much driven by the market. Bars and restaurants are constantly opening up offering different or new products. And it's basically like keeping up with the Joneses and stuff. It's like trying to see what people want now, and trying figure out what they'll want tomorrow. On top of that, we have to see what we're doing wrong and try to continue to improve on that stuff. And then keeping things updated, and repaired. New barstools, new tables, new flooring, new menus, I've*

entrepreneurs

replaced the bar top several times, and customers like seeing all those things.

It becomes a very slippery slope when you're talking about the levels of investment you put into a bar or restaurant and how you manage your inventory and signing big contracts. And when there are places opening up at a much quicker pace, the longevity of your average establishment continues to shrink every year. That's a direct result of trying to manage the human factor on how customers choose the next trends. I mean you drink mostly the same thing when you come in, and even a customer as consistent as you, you'll cycle through the beers we bring in, or you've found a couple really good ciders or whiskeys that we've added. If you drink 10 different things as a regular customer, imagine trying to manage a customer who wants to try something new every week. Keeping track of that is part of the business.

A few years ago, if you had a good gastropub you had a solid 10 years before you have to think about maybe doing some hardcore renovations and updating. If you're lucky you could push that out to maybe like 12 years. Nowadays the market's so tough if you get six years in you've got to start looking at renovating. Now you've got to put out another chunk of cash to refresh the whole place and stuff. And it's just the amount of money that has to keep getting put back into the business, back into your establishment it's doubled. And it's narrowing down the returns we can get.

But yeah, it's difficult to manage and maintain that operation cycle, and then track the changes in customer demand, and keep an eye on wider trends in the industry.

entrepreneurs

Diageo buying up one of your previous smaller brands, does that mean now your rep is going to change? And maybe how they do billing is going to change as well. You might not be able to carry your most popular craft beer because they only sell that in certain markets now. Little stuff like that.

Carlos: What do you think the biggest challenge from yourself is?

Charlie Collazo: *The biggest challenge from myself? I guess learning to accept failures and mistakes a little better. Recognizing sooner when something's not gonna work out and stuff. I will hold onto things and drag things out longer than I probably should. In anticipation of trying to make certain things work. That's probably one of my blind spots from a business sense. Not necessarily being able to cut and run. Learning when to adjust sooner than when I do or not allowing my emotional attachment to the places I build to become a factor. Yeah.*

Carlos: Did you have any mentors when you first got into this?

Charlie Collazo: *The people I worked for doing the part time side job stuff, at the time they owned the Palmer Club. They owned Woody's, and then Voyeur. They also had at the time 8th Street Lounge. In my side gig doing the lighting installs, and then eventually operating the systems as well. So doing the lights for them and interacting with them, getting to know them and each of their clubs, I got to see a lot of things that go on in the background as far as how a bar or a restaurant operates from a business perspective. It's kind of funny because after seeing all the stuff in the background, and all the dealings, and all the frustrations,*

entrepreneurs

and all the risks, and what you had to do, I wanted nothing to do with the industry. And somehow I still wound up here.

It was very eye-opening. I was always pretty grounded with kids and marriage and stuff and that was kind of rare in the nightclub end of things. There were a lot of times that I was just sitting in the office, and a high portion of people in the business, as far as staff, or owners, a lot of them are into the club drugs. A lot of times they're doing one drug or another and just a lot of unnecessary drama.

But they always knew I was pretty grounded. That stuff was never my thing anyway even before my kids. So a lot of times when they were having these really important meetings and things where they would normally be throwing other people out of the office they would have me stay just to sit there. Because they knew I was grounded and I was stable. I wasn't someone who was doing drugs or involved in all that. They knew I had my regular job at Home Depot. And a lot of times I just sat there and listened. And it was just all kinds of things. Anything from dealing with the city, to dealing with liquor companies, taxes, payroll, employees, you name it I heard all of it.

So there was a lot of great information I was able to absorb just by sitting there, shutting up, and listening. It was huge getting that type of help from them. It helped me from day one, when I first opened my place having some of the industry knowledge, some of the basics. Knowing what I was gonna have to deal with as far as different licensing from the city goes, payroll taxes, and so forth.

Carlos: That's amazing that you were able to see all of that firsthand. Get all that experience that you wouldn't get in

entrepreneurs

business school. That's the kind of stuff you have to just go through, and experience as a business owner. It's like you were able to take a class on all those things. That's great. You talked about your employees a little bit. What's the most challenging part about having employees?

Charlie Collazo: *I guess one of the most difficult things about having employees, for most people anyway, is remembering that they are people. It's like business owners can forget that part. A lot of times a manager or owner, they think of an employee as an emotionless robot or something. I think we'd all do better if we remembered we're all just people trying to get by. We're going to make mistakes and as long as you are willing to own up to it, and try to learn from it, it's probably not that big of a deal.*

It's hard firing people and stuff, because at the end of the day that person has got their bills to pay. And you know that person, and especially true for small business is you're probably friends with them or at least know about their lives. It's a lot tougher to fire a person if you know that means their kids might not eat. Granted, there are times when it's very justifiable in terminating someone but it doesn't make it easy. It doesn't mean it's easy. It's still hard. It's still a person, despite all their faults.

And then there's stuff that's associated with that. Not socially interacting with employees and stuff. It gets very difficult and it's a slippery slope when you have a small staff, and you get to know your employees and you become that friendly with them. But you also still have to be their employer and manage their schedule, and be that leader. And that might mean you have to reprimand people, or correct them when they're doing things not appropriate for a

entrepreneurs

workplace. I can't have employees giving away inventory or taking home liquor and stuff. But owners are people too, and most people will typically tend to form bonds with employees. You form those interpersonal bonds with employees since it's a smaller team. When you've got a bigger workforce, that closeness gets diluted down just due to number. The time you can spend with any single employee shrinks.

Staffing is extremely tough, particularly in this industry, and especially with cooks. Every cook thinks they're now a chef de cuisine. We'd like to get the best chefs we can but realistically we need line cooks who are competent and want to get some resume experience. This is never going to be a Michelin star restaurant. We're a bar. We're doing catfish bites, and fries, and tots. So finding a good fit for what our menu is can be a difficult balance between talent and "good enough."

Finding good bartenders can be a challenge. More accurately the issue is finding the right bartender. There's so many bartenders in the city and you can get anyone to tend bar and stuff. I can pretty much teach anyone to tend bar. The physical part of bartending isn't difficult. It's mixing some drinks, opening beers. Anyone with a pulse can do it. What is tougher to find, and really difficult to train someone to do is to socially interact. You've either got that, or you don't. That's the biggest thing. That's the most important part. For me it's how people interact with the clientele because that's what keeps drawing people back.

If people had a pleasant time they're like, "oh my God, that bartender was so cool."

Or, "he was so funny."

entrepreneurs

Even if the service wasn't great they sort of dismiss that part. They can overlook the service being so-so because they had an enjoyable time. So with the staffing that's huge. Because that's your front of house, that's the face that people see, that and your servers. That's what customers are being exposed to and that's what can make or break whether a customer is gonna come back or not. And as a business owner you want good customers who want to keep coming back.

And then as far as what are some of the enjoyable things about staff, or about employees? I would say it is forming those bonds with them. Forming a good working team and really developing a friendship with the employees here and there is really amazing. Getting to know them and their families and their kids and whatever else it may be. Just interacting with them it's great.

Carlos: You talked about your mentors when you were first starting out. Do you talk to anybody now in terms of seeking business advice?

Charlie Collazo: Yeah. There are a couple of other business owners I really go to when I need advice. I mean I've gotten to know a lot of owners and I'm friends with them. But there are two in particular that I really look to, and talk with when it comes to business and strategy and so forth. One friend is the owner of Race Street Café, and Goat Hollow. He's who is actually gonna wind up being my partner when we move The Institute down the block. There's also the primary owner of Whetstone, and Brauhaus Schmitz. He's the other owner I go to consistently.

entrepreneurs

The three of us have actually become really good personal friends and stuff. We do things socially like on a regular basis. And it's really great to have that support and that outlet with them. I feel extremely lucky knowing them because getting to talk with them, when there's situations that I may be dealing with that I've never dealt with before, and then I get input from them.

If I haven't had an experience or seen a situation before, they probably have. And vice versa. There are things they didn't know and then I may be like, "hey, you know, you can do this with the city," or whatever. And even better when you have that type of trust and that good of a relationship with other business owners, it's like a team. So when you have that good of a team to turn to, and none of you have seen something or gone through something before, you can all work together to come up with a good solution and then come back and share that with everyone. So, it's really good having that and being able to communicate with them regularly. And we're sharing a lot of other information from different sources that we know individually. Depending on what the issue is we can pool that information to get a better picture of what's going on.

Carlos: Did you know them before you opened The Institute, or did you meet them after?

Charlie Collazo: *I met one after I had opened. The other I actually met just before we opened the Institute. It turned out he was our neighbor on the same lot. It was a small, small world. Neither of us had any idea. I was doing construction and renovation for The Institute when he came through and I met him for the first time. I was talking and let him know I lived right around the corner on 11th Street*

entrepreneurs

and he started talking about how he was looking to do something, and was just about to open his first place.

And he says, "that's kind of funny, dude. I live on 11th Street also."

So it turns out we lived two blocks away from each other. We didn't even know it.

Carlos: You mentioned you live pretty close to where you opened your business. How long have you lived in Philly? How much has the city changed during that time?

Charlie Collazo: *My entire life. So that's gonna be, 47 years this year. The changes are insane. I think one of the funnier stories I tell people, and a lot of people don't believe it, but when I was growing up I can remember being like nine or ten years old and when it got dark in center city, you got the hell out. Like that movie with Will Smith, I Am Legend. Go inside, lock the doors, and duck. It was the equivalent of being in North Philly at like 8th and Butler. It was that dangerous. There was no difference.*

Center city was very, very bad and very run-down. You had Market Street which was filled with porn theaters, drugs, prostitutes, murders, gang violence. You name it. All of it. It was all very, just seedy, and violent, and so forth. So the changes I've seen like in my lifetime are staggering.

What's interesting though is those same changes and how they've revitalized the city, and now the city is going through a boom, and the people, the influx of people that are moving to the city, I feel sort of disenfranchised from the city. Because when I grew up you knew all the people on your block. You knew people on the block behind you. You knew people on the block over. You knew people two blocks

entrepreneurs

over. You knew the people in your neighborhood, in your area, not just the block.

Now Philadelphia is much more transient. You have people on blocks that don't even know any of their neighbors. Not just renters, not just students, but people buying homes and living there. And because people are just coming and going and so forth, I feel like it's, it's just very different. Philly's slogan has always been, "The City of Brotherly Love." But it's like I feel that's really changing. I mean you just don't feel that connection to your community anymore. The city used to be very connected. It's not like that anymore. It's not like it once was. It's really becoming like some of the other bigger, urban cities. Like New York, and DC, and so forth.

So, three years ago we moved out to the Manayunk section of Philadelphia. There were a couple little minor reasons here and there. One, we were kind of backed up on our home. We were still financially struggling with our mortgage because we pulled out so much equity out of the property. And then with establishing the business, it definitely hurt us. I couldn't afford to keep the home since the bar was also tied into some of the financials, in terms of loan guarantees with the bank. So that's one of the reasons we basically had to get rid of our home at the time to kind of reduce my monthly overhead as far as our mortgage.

We knew we wanted to stay in the city. The interesting thing was I was never really a fan of Manayunk because it was always associated with bros, and other douchebags. This perception was mostly because of Main Street with all the bars and restaurants there. That's where everyone hung out, and then all the college kids, and that

entrepreneurs

younger immature crowd drinking until they're puking on the corner, and peeing in the street, and so forth. But it's actually changed quite a bit. I mean you still get some of that clientele up there. But it's that appearance or that stereotype. When all you ever see is the main strip there, and you don't really look anywhere else, you don't realize how much more there is to it.

But our priority was school for our kids, and we found an amazing place where the school for our kids was literally right behind the house. And it was it is a really great, great school. And it's a Philadelphia public school. And it's just a beautiful campus. And the school attendance was well below what it was built for because the neighborhood had changed. And what Manayunk over the years or over the decades had become was very different than what this school was originally built for. If you look at Manayunk today you have more young professionals and college kids that are up there living, and renting. Manayunk isn't really a family neighborhood anymore, or at least not as much as it used to be. That means the school's attendance is half of what it was made for and it works out great for our kids. There was no problem getting my kids in the right classrooms, with good teachers. Of course the kids hated the idea of going from one school to another. They have all their friends and their social lives. But after the first year they adjusted pretty well and they realized how much better it was being up there. They really loved the change once they saw the result.

So that was big. That was really huge. And it was a bonus for us because being able to have them in public schools, and a really good public school and not having to

entrepreneurs

pay for private school helped tremendously with the financial burden of living closer to center city. So many of the schools there are just awful. War zones really.

And there were other little amenities being up there. Parks and jog trails and all that stuff. Things you'd like to have near your home. It worked out great.

Carlos: So you're married and you have five kids. Did you have all five kids when you started with the Institute? What obstacles or difficulties did you have owning and operating a business and having a large family?

Charlie Collazo: *Yeah. We actually had our fifth when we started the process to buy the bar. It was very difficult trying to like balance work and home life especially with a newborn. And it's still difficult to this day. Because we're not in a 9 to 5 business we're in a business that primarily operates from like 4pm to 2am. Our hours are completely different than a regular kid's schedule even for just something simple as daycare or school. Our off hours are different from when the kids are home you know.*

So it's tough especially when both parents are involved in the business. If it was just one of us that would be one thing there would always be at least one parent there in sync with that schedule. But when you have both parents heavily involved in getting the business moving it gets difficult trying to make sure someone is there. And at some point there will be a time when neither parent is physically there. There are times when neither one of us is there. That's when your support network becomes so crucial. It's a big help with trying to take care of things for the kids. Making sure they have lunches ready for school and that dinner is ready when they get home. Before we

entrepreneurs

have to leave to take care of the bar all those pieces have to be in place. So whether I'm coming down for the day to do maintenance, or paperwork or whatever, or coming down for the night bartend, I have to have all of that planned out or be able to adjust to make sure all those things happen before I leave. It gets really tricky, and if I'm being completely truthful a lot of times it's not really fair to the kids.

But my parents, and my family, my sister-in-law, they've all helped. A lot. That support network, without them we wouldn't have made it. Just things like watching kids here and there, or taking them for a weekend, depending on what big events we have going on. And my wife's mother lived with us for a while. In fact the first seven years of The Institute, before we moved to Manayunk, she actually lived with us. That was definitely helpful with both of us like working all the time. At least she was there.

Carlos: It's great that you have such a strong family connection and they were able to help out like that. You talked about having your wife as a part of the business as well. What's it like working with family? That's gotta provide its own unique set of challenges and opportunities.

Charlie Collazo: *It can be great. And it can be a nightmare. It's both all at the same time. Within the same moment it's both, it can be both. It's very helpful when you have that support, especially if your wife is in it, and she's in the trenches with you. She understands why you do certain things and why you're working 18 hour days. That understanding and that empathy is great. Having someone*

<u>entrepreneurs</u>

on your team you can really trust and depend on. That's really great. Knowing we both want the bar to succeed, that's really great. So there are a lot of really great things about working with your spouse that you can't get when you have separate jobs and stuff.

On the other side of that coin, when you have a personal issue or a work-related issue, there's no separation. A personal issue becomes a work issue. A work issue becomes a personal issue. Things that may be a personal problem at home spill into work and that is very messy. And then you have work problems that spill into home and become personal issues and now the family is involved because there is no separation.

People don't think about it often but one of the benefits, one of those small things about having a normal job allows is that if you work 40 hours a week, it's your separation from your significant other or your family which gives you a mental break. You get to decompress. You get a chance to step back, look at the situation objectively and then come back to those conversations with a different perspective.

Maybe recognize where you were wrong or where you didn't communicate an idea clearly, sometimes you need that alone time to really think about what your wife or husband has to say, and really consider their feelings and their opinions outside of that emotional moment when you're arguing. If I had a time to sort out all those thoughts, like time that a regular job would give me, to distract me, and I could see things clearer or understand my wife better. Or if she did a regular thing work wise, it's would give her the same thing.

entrepreneurs

Carlos: As an outsider, I will say it looks like you've managed to make it a success. You've also worked with other family members as well. I think your brother has worked here. I know your wife's brother worked here for a bit. How is that? What are some of the challenges that come with managing loved ones?

Charlie Collazo: *That's also very, very difficult. A lot of times I've brought family members on board and given them a job because they're at a tough point in their life. And sometimes they can't get beyond their issue, or where they're at in life at that point. And then I have to deal with firing them. It's already hard enough firing a regular employee but imagine you need to get rid of your sister, the kid you grew up with, because they stole from you. Or when you have to talk about firing a relative with your wife because they are dealing drugs out of the kitchen that blood tie adds another level. Now it's much more difficult because now you really know that person and have a personal connection with them because they're a family member and so forth. That's really tough. Now after you have to fire them, you still have to see them because they're family. So things can get weird at Christmas or at your mom's birthday or whatever family events are going on. It all just adds a different level to things and it's a situation you really have to think about when you make the decision to bring them into your business.*

On the other side of that coin, it's also great when you have a brother or whoever working with you because you may not normally see them, or at least not regularly. But to be able to see your brother, or your cousin, or your family on a slightly more regular basis, it's nice. And

entrepreneurs

typically, most times at least, I'm not going to say all the times, because there have been times when family members screw over family members just like anyone else, but typically your family member that's working for you is trying to look out for you also.

Carlos: Was there ever a moment in the past nine years that you thought you should just toss in the towel and quit?

Charlie Collazo: *Yeah. Let's see. I've lost count how many times. Every time there's a hard time you think, "This is it. I can toss in the towel and just be done. That's it, I quit." Or it's like that slow, damning realization of, "What have I done?" I've just financially like risked everything. I have, at least financially, potentially screwed my family over and I've thought I just need to offload this and be done. I couldn't even tell you how many times. It's well into the hundreds over the past 9 years.*

But then you come to your senses and realize how great it is being your own boss, and in charge of your own destiny, and so forth. And that's the payoff for me. Those are the times when you think you will never quit no matter wha - you'll just get up and try this stuff again. And there are hundreds of those moments too. And as long as those good moments outweigh the moments I feel like I should walk away, I'll keep doing this. I'll keep building and going and moving.

Carlos: As we've discussed, your business is in Philadelphia. What do you think makes Philadelphia unique in terms of small businesses, and that community surrounding small business owners you talked about?

entrepreneurs

Charlie Collazo: *I actually think it's losing some of its uniqueness if I'm being completely honest. I think in this city once upon a time, the small businesses and neighborhood businesses were much more integrated into and involved with their neighborhoods. The way the city has changed like how I talked about before, I don't really see that as often. You know? Added to that is the barrier of what it costs to start a business in the city now. You just can't do it with like some equity you're pulling out of your home. The financial risk is too great. You can't finance a business on your hopes and dreams. Now you need investors. Now that's another voice in how things get done.*

So, typically what you're seeing in the city now is most of the mom-and-pop stores are gone. The corner stores and bodegas in the city are dying. There are still some things like bars and restaurants can shoestring it. But you find those things more in certain districts in the city. And more and more even those corner places are also starting to require much heavier levels of investment. And even then I don't see, or I don't feel that connection with neighborhoods like there once was. You're not seeing people open corner stores anymore. Now it's a CVS or whatever.

Carlos: I don't think people hear about that very often. It's definitely an interesting perspective. One of the things you talked about that was changing in the city was how costly it's becoming to start a business.

When you were first getting started you talked about pulling out equity from your home. Did you have to go to a bank to set up a small business loan?

Charlie Collazo: *Basically I pulled out the equity through our one lender because at the time our house was basically*

entrepreneurs

paid for. I really didn't have or I didn't owe anything substantial against it. We were fortunate. But in that timeframe of all the years of living in the house the neighborhood started really developing and blowing up. So the value of my house went up. Like way up. This allowed me to pull out the majority of the money that I needed to purchase the bar. I still had to get another loan for it. And that's where things got really tough because banks will not lend you money for bars and restaurants. They have the highest failure rates among all small businesses.

So typically what people have to do is you have to seek out private lenders. And when you're seeking out private lenders, you're also paying a lot higher interest rates. Once again makes it even tougher for you to succeed. Because, you know, you could be paying several hundred to several thousand extra a month because of that private lender. So it becomes another real tough barrier, and just one more thing to overcome. Depending on what it is you're doing.

Carlos: When you started did you have any outside investors that you needed to bring on?

Charlie Collazo: *When I first started, no. About three months in, I had a friend who came in and invested as a minority shareholder. They came in at 15% because we needed the extra capital to work with when we decided to start renovating the second floor, and at the same time we saw the opportunity to expand the kitchen into the basement, open up a lot more bar space and significantly increase our ability to generate revenue.*

It helped in the beginning but they didn't have the knowledge base to really be involved in the business. They

entrepreneurs

were supposed to come in and have some limited involvement and start learning things about how to run a bar, how to do some of the functional level things like bartend. At the end of the day, it wound up evolving into just being a silent partner. I didn't envision our partnership that way, but they had a different viewpoint that didn't really match what I had in mind so in the end it didn't work out for either party.

I would have rather seen it as a situation where they were being more involved, but that's also contingent on the fact that they spend the time needed to learn the business the right way. Taking the time and getting a better understanding and firm grasp of the service industry. But they just weren't getting that. Their understanding of all of that stuff never progressed. After that I preferred them to be silent on decisions because at that point, you just become more of a hindrance than anything.

Carlos: What one piece of advice would you give to a person looking to start a business tomorrow?

Charlie Collazo: *I'd want them to really, really, really do the homework for whatever it is they are going to try and do. Don't just do something based on a dream. Don't just jump into it blindly. There's nothing wrong with dreaming and trying to live that dream. But not preparing for that dream can hurt you badly. And it if you haven't done the proper foundational work, the proper research, it'll hurt worse. If you haven't done the proper research, you might as well throw your money away.*

Knowing the neighborhood is super important. I think it's something that gets overlooked a lot. Knowing the area where you're going into and knowing what the

entrepreneurs

demographics are like. Do the people, do they really want what you're thinking you're going to do? Because it's a much higher level of investment when you're talking about a bar and restaurant especially now so you want to do as much of that homework I talked about, do as much of that as you can before you jump in.

You really have to have a long-term game plan. You also have to have a plan in place if your business isn't successful. Are you prepared to struggle and float this business for five years? What about ten years? If it's something you're gonna be relying on to help support your family you really need to have not just a plan A - you have to have plan B through Z. What happens if the business isn't doing exactly what you thought? What if you're not making any money because you overestimated your margins? Or you have to put in $2,000 every month to keep this business operating until it materializes over the next 6 months because your growth projections were off by 3%. Think about that.

So it's not just a matter of having a business plan. I think that's one of the big things that gets missed when they talk about having a business plan. You can't, or you shouldn't just go in with a single business plan. You need several business plans. You need to think about different scenarios of things not going how you expected. You have to have all your contingencies. It's just like the military. The military goes in and has a battle plan, but they have several battle plans in place when they going in. Because it's like what happens if this happens, or this happens instead, or this other thing we didn't think would be an issue happens.

entrepreneurs

Philadelphia in particular I don't feel is a, which they claim they are, but I don't feel it's a friendly for small businesses. Financially, they've made it very difficult to succeed. There's so much that's required now, so much red tape. Between all the various construction permits, and zoning requirements, and licenses for tying your shoes. It's not as easy as pulling out equity from your house to do like a small little mom-and-pop shop. I mean, depending on what you're doing, you have to think about having team of investors. Not just to mitigate risk but to even be able to pool enough capital.

I mean even take like a small shop, or even just a freakin' ice cream stand, that could easily cost you more than $50,000 in the city right now. And it's always a nice thought of having your own business and it's just you. But you really have to think about maybe taking on a partner regardless how small the business is. Because as great as the success may be, there's also the flip side that if it's not as successful, and it's going to take you time, you're not bearing 100% of the burden. And you're not risking your family as harshly if things fail. If you have someone else involved with you that risk goes down so those are a lot of things to like think about when undertaking a bigger business when starting a new venture.

Carlos: Any hazards or dangers you would want people to know about that maybe you wished you knew before you started?

Charlie Collazo: *Be careful when dealing with private lending. That's a big, big issue depending on what type of rate you're gonna get from a private lender. You have to be careful of that. Like just in the nine years since I started my*

entrepreneurs

bar, the cost of opening up a new bar is almost double because of the value of liquor licenses. My first purchase, the Institute cost me $335,000. And over time I've spent probably about another $150,000 on everything. Equipment, renovations, licenses, all that stuff. Actually it may be more than that maybe closer to $200,000 over the nine years on all kinds of things. Plus when we decided to add a real kitchen in the basement was more. But let's say at the end of the day it cost around $535,000 total cash investment. Going to a private investor can be very attractive way to raise funding.

Especially now. Today you're looking at probably closer to about $800,000 maybe $850,000. Somewhere in that range to do something depending on what your idea is for your place, buying a liquor license, buying the property.

Carlos: Looking back on when you first started, what was the most difficult decision you made that has had the longest term impact for you?

Charlie Collazo: *We bought our property. I mean that's the biggest difference between most bars or restaurants that start. I own my property. I own the bricks. Where probably 75% of the places in the city as far as bar and restaurants go, those places usually don't own their bricks. They're just renting. It's very difficult. The decision to by the property put me at a great advantage long term but I am also very lucky in how the neighborhood turned out.*

In the beginning if you're just renting you don't have as much on the line because you haven't just purchased a property. When you buy the bricks, then there's all the maintenance you have to worry about with that property. All the things that need to be done like fixing the furnace,

entrepreneurs

getting a new AC, or if there's a plumbing problem, congratulations hope you're a plumber because it's going to cost you or you'll have to shut down. You can't operate without a working toilet. Eventually you will hit a crossroad that it becomes beneficial to owning. There are definitely huge benefits for you when you finally own the property. But just like everything else with business there's risk involved and money. So in the beginning if it's a leased space, it's beneficial to the person that's renting. Your costs won't be as much to start. But when you start getting beyond five years that's when things start to change. That cost benefit starts to change where now it becomes beneficial to own the building and you're wishing you could have bought the property instead of lease.

For me it's worked out pretty good because I bought my property when it was in an up and coming neighborhood. The neighborhood is now booming. A tremendous amount of construction has happened. All kinds of building has been going on from residential to new commercial space, and some of the old abandoned manufacturing spaces are being turned into apartments and condos. So the property value here has doubled in nine years. That's crazy to think about. And that has allowed me to do this move into the new location, which is an old manufacturer they're renovating into a mixed use.

Carlos: Operationally how does owning versus leasing make a difference in the long term; is it just the money aspect or are there other considerations?

Charlie Collazo: *The money is a big part of it especially long term. With owning your bricks it's a bigger upfront expense because you're talking about getting loans to buy*

entrepreneurs

the property and so forth. But no matter what your mortgage is gonna stay the same. But from an operating viewpoint let's say you hit that 5 year mark, and you have a successful business and you go back to renegotiate your new lease. Well now you're a successful business. Now you're gonna get hammered on your rent. And you're going to have to pay those increases every time because part of your identity as a bar and restaurant is your location. Picking up and moving can have a huge impact outside of the disruption to sales. Even if you are financially able to do it moving your bar can dramatically alter the identity of your bar and upset your regular customer base.

It's very, very rare that you have an opportunity to move it where it's not gonna be harmful to the business. And the property owner knows that and they're going to use that to leverage higher and higher rent. Now your profits are going to get eaten up by someone else who wasn't a part of your business. That's something to consider when evaluating the competition in a neighborhood. Maybe you'll be able to afford a price war in five years when your competition is renegotiating their lease and their rent is gonna go up your mortgage is still the same. So those are some things you can think about when you're deciding to buy or own that are outside of the financial impacts.

Carlos: Can you talk a little bit about what your best experience has been with the Institute?

Charlie Collazo: *I think the best experience I've had is creating our pumpkin event. It's hell to pull off. And for as much as I bitch about it, and I don't get to sleep for days, it's also the most fun I have all year. So that's one thing I*

entrepreneurs

really like take pride in and I love doing. It's funny it started off basically nine years ago. At the time we were just constantly trying to think of just fun, quirky, different types of events to do and way to be different than an average corner bar. And we were looking for different style beer events that no one was really doing yet. So we're like, "wow, no one's really doing a pumpkin beer event in Philadelphia." So we decided to do a pumpkin beer event.

That first Saturday the event was supposed to be starting at 2pm. And I got over here at like 12pm to open the bar and there was I think there were probably about 12 people waiting in line.

And I said, "you know, we don't, we don't open up for a little bit." Then I remembered the pumpkin event and I asked, "are you guys here for the pumpkin event?"

And they said, "yeah."

I'm like, "well we don't open for a little bit but if you wanna go around the corner Prohibition Taproom is open. If you wanna get something to drink while you are waiting or something." Just trying to be friendly send some business to a friend, get them out of the cold.

And they're like, "no. We'll wait. It's fine."

And that's when I realized holy shit, we're gonna get slammed. There are people here like waiting already, and we're not even open yet. This is crazy. And it wasn't supposed to be anything big. I think we had like eight pumpkin beers or nine pumpkin beers that first year. And we got rocked. We filled up the first floor. We filled up the second floor. It ended up being a really great success. Everyone had a really great time.

entrepreneurs

Flash forward 5 years and things were just over-the-top. We had the whole street shut down a full city block from 11th street to 12th street. It was packed inside, outside, everywhere. There was pumpkin beer pouring everywhere. The whole freakin' street smells like damn cinnamon and nutmeg. It was nuts. There were food vendors with pumpkin themed food. Ice cream, street food, all of it was pumpkin.

So that's definitely the most enjoyable event because for as much work as it is, it's always such a great feeling when you have customers telling you, "dude, I've been here four years in row."

"I've been here five years in a row."

"I've been here every year. I love your pumpkin festival."

It's a great feeling when you have customers, like I said earlier, they're looking for you and they're engaging you and giving you feedback.

And it's also one of the funnier things because I've got people walking up to me, and they're like, "Hey, Charlie, how's it going? Oh, dude, I love you man."

Okay, nice. Internally I'm thinking, "who was that? I've never seen that person before in my life!" People know who I am because of the event but I've got no clue who they are. You're cordial because they're customers but when you get like halfway through that day, and everyone's trashed and slurring, and there's over 2500 people there, the last thing you wanna be doing is talking to like a thousand drunken people and stuff. And you just can't remember all of them.

entrepreneurs

I don't know how it's gonna be this year. It was at one point the largest pumpkin beer event in the country, at least. The funny thing is we always say the country, and then one of our friends actually pointed out that well it's technically the biggest pumpkin beer event in the world. Nobody does pumpkin beer events anywhere in the world and stuff. That's a U.S. thing.

One day he said, "so you can pretty much safely say you're the biggest in the world."

So that's worked out great for us. It's something we really enjoy doing. It's been a beast to pull off, but yeah, it's been very successful for us.

Carlos: That's amazing. So that's been the best experience. Let's pivot and look at what's been the worst experience you've had.

Charlie Collazo: *The worst experience I've had here? Oh boy. Let me think. I would say it's something that's more of a financial issue than anything else between dealing with the city, having some tough years here and there. Just falling back in bills and not being able to pay my mortgage thinking, "oh my God. Am I going to lose my house?" There have been very stressful times - not days, not weeks, but months and months. And then more months of stress like that. The financial worries and hardship has been the most stressful thing.*

I think my family is what drives that. It would be one thing if I wasn't married and didn't have kids. I could suck it up and not a big deal. If I'm a single guy and I'm gonna be able to go on and get a job. But I need to be able to provide housing for my family and my kids. I still have to feed them and take care of them. So it's a lot scarier when

entrepreneurs

you have people that are dependent on you in that capacity. But that stress, those thoughts, that's what has been the worst to experience as a business owner. Just that feeling like it might happen, or it could happen.

Carlos: So you mentioned early on that you were an operations manager at Home Depot. You had direct reports. What do you think the biggest difference is going from managing people that you are not financially responsible for to managing people who you are now financially responsible for as their employer?

Charlie Collazo: *One of the hardest things as far as like employing people is being able to pay those people. Knowing these people are working for you and counting on you. And there are times, especially during the summer months, when you hit really bad, tough stretches. So it's like you're doing everything you can to reduce cost of your overhead. And that typically means looking at your biggest expense. And for most small businesses your biggest expense is your payroll.*

So trying to minimize that without fully eliminating the normal positions you have. But then panic mode kicks in because you have those weeks where you're thinking oh my God I can't pay my employees this week. I'm supposed to be cutting them checks on Friday. It's Monday, it's the end of the month, and we didn't hit our sales numbers this weekend. All the bills are due. It's really hard when you have to ask an employee, "hey, can you wait like two days before you cash your check?"

It's humbling. And that's very difficult and very scary for everyone. For one, it's a pride issue. Because nobody wants to be that guy that can't pay the people that work for

entrepreneurs

you. And those people, they're depending on you. You're their leader and they're expecting you to make the right decisions so they can show up to work and have a job. And it's not just them; they've all got their families. And because you know them you know their families. You know their kids, their wives, their husbands. They've got their rent and their mortgages that they have to pay as well. So, ironically, you're putting them into that awful place that you don't like and you don't wanna go through it and then you don't wanna be the cause of doing it to someone else either. It's brutal. It's heartbreaking. That's probably one of the tougher things and takes a different mentality to cope with than just managing someone for some other company.

Carlos: Do you think your experience as an operations manager with Home Depot helped you run things a little more efficiently?

Charlie Collazo: Yes and no. I think it gave me a little more of the corporate mentality for scheduling efficiency, some of the managerial thinks people don't think of, ordering bathrooms supplies, some of the logistics and stuff. But then by the same token it's a whole different type of beast. Because when you're talking about working for a large corporation like Home Depot things are very structured and very methodical in what has to be done when. Having a bar or a restaurant is not because things are just constantly flying at you. It's nonstop.

You're dealing with all kinds of things possibly breaking down. Or dealing with issues like you may not have a proper licensing on something from the city or the state, and who has jurisdiction over what license. Or there's a tax bill you've got to pay with the city, and with the state,

entrepreneurs

and with the IRS. So it's definitely tough. Like I said, it, it gave me some basic knowledge from an operational end helping me run the business. But it was still kind of like being thrown to the wolves.

Carlos: Not to cut you short but let's end with something light hearted and I'm going to put "the boss" in the hot seat a little bit, who's been the most fun to work with?

Charlie Collazo: *Oh man you're going to get me in trouble. I would say as far as one of the more fun employees to work with, it would have to be Ed. Ed's got a really, really good sense of humor about things. He's pretty damn funny. And working with him, because he can be a real big goofball and stuff, it's always a good time. I always leave in a better mood.*

He's also very talented and has that personality to be a good bartender. He is able to adjust the quickest in a social setting to customers and stuff. Depending on the customer's demeanor when they come in he's always very quick to sense how they're doing. He can definitely read the crowd. If someone comes in and they're happy, and they're excitable, he can just take it to the next level. If someone's kind of down, or grouchy, or depressed, he's able to lift their spirits a little bit. Get some jokes in there and so forth. He is very skilled at reading people, and working well in situations with customers and clientele.

take away

Earlier I mentioned the importance of establishing why your business will exist. What I learned from Charlie is that it can be just as valuable to identify exactly why

entrepreneurs

you want to start a business. This may or may not be the same as why your business exists. For Cathy her internal why and the business why are the same: help foster children. This why can be your guiding light to weather the eventual storms you'll face as a business owner.

Your why might be any number of things. Maybe you have experience in the industry you're looking to enter. You have the advantage of seeing what mistakes, or missteps another entrepreneur might be making, and where you can cut costs or improve service. You believe this experience will give you a competitive advantage and enable your success. Or that's the idea anyway.

Maybe your why is that you like the idea of the challenges you'll face (the passion we talked about earlier). Maybe it's the love of competition. Early in the conversation that's the sense I got from Charlie. He saw other people doing something and felt the challenge and competitive drive to do it better. This is one of the fundamental principles of economics: competition. Competing businesses that believe they alone can best serve a segment of a population. It's the Coke versus Pepsi mentality. Your product is better; your service is superior.

Now if you can just get it off the ground and running. And then you hit your first obstacle. The water heater in the space you're leasing goes bad and floods everything. Your landlord will cover the repair but you lost half your inventory. The insurance will cover it but you won't see that money for another 3 months during the claims process. You'll have to close for the day to clean up, and it won't be repaired until next Wednesday so you can't operate because the city mandates you have a working

entrepreneurs

water heater to meet health code standards. Now you lost a week of revenue.

Why am I doing this again? Those doubts will start to creep up. It's normal. Discovering what your motivation can help you understand why you run your own business. Is it simply for externalities like fame or fortune? Or is an internal motivation? You want to take care of your family or you love the feeling of independence or creativity that comes with operating your own business.

Often we tie ourselves to a single idea about something, be it a relationship, hobby, or the business we build. Then we try to conform our lives around that single idea. This can be an effective strategy that leads to success for many things in our lives. For an entrepreneur building a business this may present a danger. Trying to tie yourself to any single motivation may hamper long term success because that motivation may cease to be appealing to you. Your internal motivation may change, morph, or disappear entirely and make you want to quit. Or it may become multiple reasons.

Charlie's why seemed to morph as we got deeper into the interview and further along the timeline of experiences in owning and operating a business. He started with some adjacent experience in the bar industry, saw an opportunity he felt was a challenge, and was driven by competitiveness to start his own bar. Over time his why ultimately morphed into helping others. Stepping back a little I could see Charlie really feels connected with the people he gets to interact with. He provides a space people can enjoy and relax. A respite from the stress of their everyday lives. At least that's the way he made me

entrepreneurs

feel as a regular and if you ever get a chance to visit his bar and have a conversation with him, you'll hear in his voice how genuinely glad he is to meet you.

The idea of independence was also a large theme throughout the interview. This was expressed indirectly through his love for being self deterministic. His love for his family was also consistently present. Being able to not only support and care for his children but also provide a support for extended family members. He was also able to maintain healthy relationships with his family despite working long hours. His motivation, his why, was multifaceted and it morphed over time but it was clearly defined at each stage, and wholly present throughout the conversation.

A year out from the interview I thought about what I had learned from Charlie. I think the biggest thing that stuck for me was how much he truly enjoyed the day to day operations of his business. He cared about the people he interacted with and sought to balance work life and home life. For me, and many others these are critically important to find success whether you work a job you love or a start up your own company. I've experienced many leaders who simply didn't care about their team members. It showed and was felt by their teams, and was reciprocated in the work performance and engagement by the team. This is one area in which Charlie is a strong and capable leader.

I've meet many small business owners who say they spend more time working at their own business than they ever did working a typical 9-5. The difference maker for them is that they understand the hours they work directly

entrepreneurs

correlate to their success in someway. One of my favorite movies is Office Space by Mike Judge. There's a line in there where the main character talks about the fact that if he sells one more unit for the company there's no perceived benefit. While not every hour or minute spent working has the same value for an entrepreneur it's more tangible and directly correlates to the success of a business when an owner spends 60-70 hours a week working. This is contrast is particularly more evident to people working salaried positions sacrificing their health and personal life to "get ahead."

Charlie has been fortunate in that his family is tied to his business which, by his own admission can be a double edged sword. But because he genuinely cares for the people around him, his work becomes enjoyable. One of the most cliche sayings in the professional world is to "find something you love to do" and I think Charlie had done that. But I think he's also found a way to surround himself with people he likes to be around. I'm not certain if it's his nature or personality or outlook on life that enables this but the end result is that if he works an 18 hour day, he's more physically tired than mentally exhausted.

As someone who has worked 18 hour days at jobs I was particularly fond of, I often found myself more mentally exhausted from stress than the physical exhaustion of toiling for 18 hours a day at a desk doing office work, or spending 18 hours outdoors performing manual labor. Granted it's not always the case and I think it was implied in some of his stories that the stress of owning a business can be crushing if you allow it to be.

entrepreneurs

But I think all of the things Charlie talked about are important for a budding entrepreneur to understand before abandoning all responsibility and leaping into a new business. Sometimes people see their boss golfing all day, or schmoozing with clients and never in the office and think to themselves, "I can do that. I can run this company." What they don't see is the 40+ hours that owner worked that week after hours, early morning, weekends all day, away from their family and friends. And that even if you do love your work as much as Charlie or are as passionate about your mission as Cathy, at some point it's still going to be work. The real question is if that work continues to hold value for you? Is it something you don't dread doing? I learned recently I don't have to love my work, but I can't dread doing it.

entrepreneurs

Sean McDermott: Precision Mechanical

I meet Sean during grad school. It took me about a year to really get to know him. Grad school for me was more about personal growth than anything else. So when I say it took me a year to get to know him it was because for most of my life to that point, I had never taken the time to get to know very many people. It would have been more accurate to say I knew about people. But when I finally took the time to start actually engaging with individuals I quickly learned Sean is a really amazing person.

Sean is a large, intimidating man. He stands about six foot two inches, and is built like a professional wrestler. You'll often find him wearing work boots, a polo shirt, jeans, and a jeff cap. He's one of the kindest, most soft spoken and intelligent individuals you'll ever meet. He's very engaging if you allow him to be and what struck me the most about him was how curious he is about, well, everything. He wants to know you. He wants to know about you. He wants to know about the space you've create around you. He's one of the most exceptional people I know. Sorry ladies (and gentlemen) he's happily married with 3 children.

It was 10 July 2017 and I still have the appointment on my Google calendar. I don't remember our exact conversation but I do remember quite distinctly that it was a conversation with Sean over lunch at the Habit Burger on route 1 in Lawrenceville, New Jersey. We were walking to our cars and he said something that in hindsight I wish I had written down. While it was just a slight nudge his

entrepreneurs

words altered my trajectory just enough to wildly change where I saw myself in 10, 15, or 20 years.

When I finally organized my thoughts and my nerdy excitement turned to focus I knew immediately I wanted to interview him. He was a huge catalyst for sending me down my current path and below is the result. I hope you learn as much from him as I did and continue to do every time we meet. Enjoy.

entrepreneurs

ϕ

Carlos: What hit me the most was 99% of all businesses in the country are small businesses. By definition that means any employer with fewer than 500 employees. Which is a lot. 500 employees is a lot. But 89% of those, of the 99%, so basically 90% of businesses in the country, have 20 or fewer employees. There are not a lot of folks that talk about that and address the issues that a small business owner might face. I'm sure someone has done it, and done it better. More people should do it. More people should talk about the adventure of being a small business owner. More people should share their experiences, and their struggles, and tell their stories. Because I think it's valuable. I think there's wisdom and knowledge people can use.

Also I didn't want this to come off as preachy or as another how-to manual. You should do this and you need to do that. First, who am I? I'm not Elon Musk. I haven't built an empire. I'm focused more on just telling a story and providing a venue for people to share their experiences and wisdom with other entrepreneurs. I wanted to give people a platform to talk about their business, talk about their experiences with their business. To provide one more way for people to connect or to feel connected to other humans. What struggles did they have? What issues did they resolve? How did they address those issues? Talk about some of their successes. Talk about some of their failures or missteps. How did they deal with some of those things on a personal level? And by sharing those stories and enabling people to make their own connections and draw out their own lessons on what

entrepreneurs

to do and what not to do. It becomes very empowering and hopefully they feel like they can develop their own ideas on how they should run their business. And through that empowerment they feel more connected to the world around them because they belong to this community of entrepreneurs. Like you know what, I'm going through the same thing right now, I read this and I feel better about it. That's the zone that I want to be in. That's the concept.

And rather than try and summarize all those stories into step by step lessons just go straight to the source. You know more about what you've done, and I think that's the thing that people forget a lot of the time. I haven't lived your life. I don't know what experiences you've had. You've run a business for the past 10 years, I haven't. I want to leverage that. I want to know what lessons I can learn from you, so I don't make those same mistakes. It's kind of what our program taught me. Just walking into situations with the attitude that I'm a dummy, and I don't know anything, and I want to learn as much as possible from everyone else because they're always going to know something I don't.

The biggest thing business school taught me is that I don't know what I'm doing. But everything I set out to do with the program, I've done, and now it's just a matter of how to implement that knowledge and that experience and that growth into whatever I'm going to do next. So I'm just going to find the smartest people I can, and do what they tell me to do. I'm going to model my decisions after them, and try to do something useful, not just for me, but for the community at large. And that's what we're here doing. I hope.

entrepreneurs

Sean McDermott: *The reason we're sitting here today is because you picked me out of a hat.*

Carlos: The reason is because you're an amazing individual. That's why we're here. I feel like since Israel I've gotten to know people a lot better. Part of that is I'm just opening up a little bit more. It takes me a while; I'm a little better now, but it takes me a while to open up to people, to spend time with them, and really get to know them.

Sean McDermott: *Emotional intelligence.*

Carlos: Yeah.

Sean McDermott: *It's, that is something that can be, and I feel like it can be acquired. Self-awareness right?*

Carlos: It's like reading. You get better at it as you do it more.

Sean McDermott: *That's true, no, that's a really good point. Yeah, you get smarter. So where did you want to start? Or did we start?*

Carlos: I kind of interrupted. I think we were on a good roll but let's just hit the basics. Your name is?

Sean McDermott: *Sean McDermott.*

Carlos: You have a business partner, and you knew him at your previous company, you guys worked together. Is it just the one business partner? Did you know him before that or did you meet him while working there?

Sean McDermott: *Yeah, just Ray. We'd known each other for about, four years. We have basically the same work ethic and Ray's about seven years, seven or eight years older than me. By far one of the best pipe fitters I've ever met in my life. And a great human being. He takes care of his family. He's a compassionate guy. He has a lot of*

entrepreneurs

incredible and good qualities. And, so it was a good partnership from the beginning.

And what I realized is he was asking for me to come on his jobs over other people who'd been there longer. And I didn't understand why. I was at that point, I think I was still an apprentice. But Ray's a really good teacher, and I believe he was teaching me part of his trade. That part of this business. My experience was more service and he's more construction. But he was showing me how to lay out pipe and how to cut valves. You know things to do that were maybe industry standard, and he was saying, there's a better way. There's a better way to do this and a better way to do this. And that's what makes him a really good mechanic. He's able to say, this is what they taught you, don't do that. You'll get better results if you do this. This is smarter, this is better. This is what's going to make the customer happier. And Ray is able to look at jobs strategically. And it was a really good fit going into business together.

Carlos: And the business the two of you own is?

Sean McDermott: *Our company is called Precision Mechanical Services. We're a mechanical contractor in Philadelphia & Tri-state area. We pride our self in working hand-in-hand with customers to mitigate risk for their equipment and come up with solutions that help the equipment run longer. Help them feel more comfortable in whole process of what we're trying to do for them. And we try to have a little extra touch where we become the subject matter expert. That's the goal to be the subject matter expert on what we actually work on.*

entrepreneurs

So the customer, when they call us, we show up, they walk away. We see their back. That's our goal. That's how we know we're doing a good job. People are looking over their shoulders, yeah, we're okay with that also. If someone's upset about a process on their end that maybe everything didn't go from A to B to C. It didn't follow that category but it went from A to D. You don't get upset about that. I'm thinking, this is why they need us. They need us there so we can string everything together and we can make sure it makes sense for them. We want them to know, we're here now. We can take care of this. We can address this. Give us a couple hours we'll have answers for you. We'll have solutions for you. And I think when you start explaining to them and the more people see that we're not just there to fix their air conditioning. We're not just there to fix refrigeration. We're not there to just throw in some piping and stuff. We're there to make a difference.

We sit down with clients and one of the things I ask them is, how can we lose your business? Not how can we get more of it, how can we lose it? And a lot of times they don't know. And I try to bring up things I think we're doing well and I ask how can we do them better.

We've been in business since 2007. My partner and I both worked for a company called, Harkins & Harkins Mechanical, which was a great mechanical contractor in the area. I believe at one point they were like top 10 mechanical contractor in the country. Just great organization but they came into some issues, some troubles I guess at some point. They just had some financial woes.

But I always wanted to start my own company, so I did. I asked Ray, to be my business partner. He took care

entrepreneurs

of the construction service side. I took care of the services and in the beginning realistically what was going to happen was I was going to inherit that chaos of working with the tools. But I made a pact with myself. In the first 15 months I was going to put the tools down.

Let me think. In the first four months, I hired my first employee. My second employee I probably hired somewhere around seven months. We hired Trish, who is our administrator, our office manager. She's everything to us. We hired her around the nine month mark in September of 2007. Then we hired one more guy. Actually in our first year we hired close to six people. So at that point I did put the tools down and I made this a legitimate business. Which was all new to me.

Now people think, well, yeah, that's pretty spectacular you did that. But there was a massive learning curve. Between working and, trying to figure out what to do, what not to do, making mistakes. Learning from the business mistakes, and becoming a better business man every day. Then on top of that I have to convince people why we're better than company A, B or C. I also had to convince the customer at some point that you don't want me working on your stuff anymore. You want these guys working on it. That was the hardest part. Convincing the customer that the people I was bringing in to do the work, they're much smarter than me.

That's type of individual that I hire. I hire people who are technically smarter than me. They're all really great human beings. You know you learn from your mistakes, also from hiring people, and I certainly have made some hiring mistakes. Who to hire. When to hire. Maybe to hire

entrepreneurs

you have to interview 10 people in order to get one. That was foreign to me.

And it is difficult I believe because I have a mindset of an engineer and how I think is long-term. I think about problem solving constantly. So I have to mend multiple mindsets together. Thinking like an engineer, thinking like a mechanic, and thinking about business development. How do we drum up business? And part of the thought process when we first went into business was the quicker I can get the tools put down the quicker I can make this into a legitimate business. And that's what we did. We started with two guys, me and my partner Ray. Now we have two part-timers, who help out, and we're at I think 30, 35 employees.

That's over like a 10 year span, and last year we did little over $8.3 million dollars. And one of the ways we did this, we wrote a piece of software in 2010, and we pushed it out in 2011. We had been looking at the way we collect and had identified our problem immediately. Our billing sucked. And the way we were getting paid was terrible. We're a company that sets terms. We give people credit. An example would be in a restaurant, we're sitting here now, this coffee, and those eggs we ate, they have 30 days to pay that stuff. But the restaurant gets paid today. Right? I buy something, I have 30 days to pay too, but I figure 45 days until I get paid. So I was constantly thinking, how do I speed that process up?

So, we looked at it and we said, "okay, how do we get better?"

And we wrote this piece of software, and at that time we had four operating cash flow cycles a year. It was

entrepreneurs

terrible. We were getting paid basically every 90 days of the year. So we're getting paid four times a year. 18 months later we were getting 15 operating cash flow cycles. Dramatically changed our business. And leading up from when we executed it, to the point where it was making a recognizable difference, was maybe three months. I remember I went to my secretary and asked her, did we pay everyone? Why do we have money in the bank? Like that was foreign to me. Why do we have money in the bank?

As you grow and every company wants same thing, growth. That's something I think most people miss. And entrepreneurs they talk about growth, and they talk about it like it's rolling a boulder up the hill and they're picking up more and more shit along the way, till you get to the top.

And then you roll it off the hill and people go, "oh now, now it's easy it's all downhill."

No, when you hit that like growth section what you realize is, all your cash disappeared.

Because you're like, "yeah, we're going to grow this year by 20%," and no one understands how to do those numbers.

What does 20% look like? What did you share that with your bank? Your bank should be your partner. Can you pay off that debt service? Where did your cash go? Is it going just for your straight up cost of goods? Or is it going towards your materials? Where's it going? Did your insurance increase? Are your operating expenses are much higher because of that? You need to look at all those little things.

entrepreneurs

And initially, growth killed us. And I think not talking to your bank or including them in your work processes is a mistake. When you go to a bank I can tell you one thing, tell them the bad news. Don't tell them the good news, they already know the good news, they can read your numbers. Tell them the bad news, be honest with them. Tell them where you're struggling because they can probably help. Cost of capital cost money. It's debt but it's better than giving up equity if you don't want to do that. So you're looking at an institution that has money, and you're a startup or you're three, four year established company that needs access to that money. Be honest with them, tell them what you need. Tell them where you're going. Hey, we have five contracts right here. We have four or five jobs that are 4 million dollars. We need to bump our line of credit up. Or ask yourself, do I need to bring in investors? This is the stuff where the leader of the business needs to be thinking about. This is why the leader of the business can't be working with the tools, you know? That's, that's how I look at it.

Carlos: How did you pick this industry? Did you fall into it? Was it just something that you knew you wanted to do?

Sean McDermott: *So we started, me and this other guy, we would do some like I guess you'd technically would call it side work. And the business side always fascinated me, and I started doing that when I was around 26. I got sober at that point, and my whole life turned around. Prior to my sober date in October 2002, I was living in the land of the dead. And I got sober and I started living in the land of the living. That's the best way to put it. It's the best way to put*

entrepreneurs

being away from substances that I was abusing; that were destroying me physically, and mentally.

When I went sober I felt like I put a pair of glasses on that for the first time and I could see things differently. I started thinking differently. And I started thinking well I can make a difference. I know that I can do X, Y and Z and I can do those things better than these other people. That's what I was telling myself internally. I wasn't sure if I could. But I did know this: I work harder than most people. Because I just won't go home. You know, when 3:30 comes around, and it didn't matter when I was working for Harkins or not I didn't go home. Work started at 7:00am leave at 3:30. But I got there quarter after 6:00 and I didn't leave sometimes till quarter after 4:00.

I knew there was stuff to get done. There was stuff to set up for the next day. And that got blended into the side work we were doing. But I started looking at the business model, and I shouldn't say business model but simple things like price, cost, and profit. And I'm thinking this is what we're going to charge. This is our cost. This is profit. It was a very simple way of looking at it. And we're not talking a lot of money here. We're talking maybe, $100 here, $100 there. But at the end of the day, that's what got me into the business. And after doing that for a while, I started thinking I'm going to go start my own company.

So I went down, we were working at a hospital, and I went to the director of the hospital at the time and I asked if I went business would they potentially give us work?

And at this point, there was really no business or anything and that individual looked at me and said,

entrepreneurs

"absolutely. When you get your business, I'll have a vendor number for you that Monday."

And that was the first time I actually felt pressure in my life. For one, I didn't want to let that person down. They are an awesome, awesome human being, and they put a lot of trust in us. And so our first stop was at this hospital and from there we went to a pharmaceutical. We went to a prestigious university. And this is kind of how we got started with Precision Mechanical Services. We knew from the very beginning what we were going to do. From the skillset that Ray had in construction services, we know that there's infrastructures in these buildings that need maintenance and they need care and they need, actually need someone to tell them that you should be doing this, this and this.

You know our, first couple jobs were putting up fences and people think like, you're a mechanical contractor, but you're putting up fences? We'd do anything we had to do. You wanted to pay me to sweep your floor, I would've swept your floor, it didn't matter. And I think that's the difference when you're, when you're an entrepreneur, maybe from being like an industrial entrepreneur instead of a tech entrepreneur. There's a, there's a massive difference.

At the end of the day I think our behaviors are different more than anything else. I think today when people read about like the tech entrepreneur they think glitz, glam, high exits. But that's not always the reality. I think you only hear about the good stories. They should start publishing all the bad things because they would have people stop, maybe pursuing that. And maybe, maybe look

entrepreneurs

back on things that maybe the American public or maybe even international public really need.

Maybe they need a better coffee cup, right? Something people need that people use all the time. I'm not saying you need a better coffee cup. There are things that are out there that have revolutionized the world, that you use every day and you don't even realize how much went into it. You think this is just simple idea, or thing. But some brilliant entrepreneur came up with that idea. Or it came from someone who's working at a company who is an intrapreneur. Did that answer your question?

Carlos: That's good. These are good answers man. So you talked a little bit about how you started, where you came from. Kind of what your overall goal for your business is. What is your favorite thing about owning a business? What gets you excited about having your own business. Making your own way.

Sean McDermott: *I think the freedom. If I was working for someone. If I had an idea and I brought it to my manager. They might not accept it. They might think it's a bad idea because they think it's a bad idea. Not because it's a bad idea for the business, but they think it might misrepresent their mission or their vision. And in the past, I have brought up different ideas, at other places I worked at and they never left the room. My boss, or supervisor, or manager would listened to me, and they wouldn't give me any feedback, and they would just do the nod and smile. I'm not sure they were in the right position anyway but they were more or less sounding boards and the ideas would end right there.*

entrepreneurs

Entrepreneurship is powerful. That's how I look at it, and it's given me freedom and it's given me constraints. It's given me a way of life that is very nice. But I work really hard. You have to work really hard. So being an entrepreneur the ideas that I have, I have the ability to flesh them out. Thinking, and talking with other entrepreneurs. Running it through people who are employed by me. Talking to other entrepreneurs who have no business dealings at all in my business but will give me honest feedback. I think coming up with ideas, and I do, I come up with a ton of ideas all the time. Some good, some bad. That's the best part, that I actually have somewhere to take them. They don't have to go to the graveyard. These ideas can be brought forward and explored and I can use the tools of capital budgeting to see if they make sense or not financially. We learned in business school that, just because something you choose, that it's maybe a bad idea from a net present value perspective, is not necessarily a bad idea. It's just a bad idea financially. Long-term though, if you push it out x amount of years, it might look different.

I think that and the fact that I've got to meet some extraordinary people. That I would never be able to meet if I wasn't an entrepreneur. I get to travel some really cool places. I get exposed to things that I never would of got exposed to. I never would of went to business school if I wasn't an entrepreneur. Because I wouldn't of had an entrepreneur's organization in my life, and I wouldn't of had the 10,000 small businesses in my life, and I wouldn't of had one of the main guys there to question me, why I didn't get my MBA. If I wasn't in business and wasn't an entrepreneur I never would have met my business mentor,

entrepreneurs

who has really constructed how I think. And pushing me to challenge myself every day, in a lot of different ways. And he doesn't even know it.

So being an entrepreneur on the surface is one thing and we're not talking about running your business but like the exposure that it has for you outside of that. If you allow it to happen. There's how do I say it? Intrinsic benefits that you get. There's things that I never would have experienced if I wasn't an entrepreneur. It was the best decision I made. The scariest decision I ever made. Starting my own company.

I remember when I started. I remember my face broke out for almost like three weeks. And this stress that I felt that I was under. Because I knew I couldn't, I wasn't going backwards. I wasn't. I wasn't going to go and work for someone. If this just didn't work out I was going to try again, and again, and again. I just wasn't going to be defeated. But the amount of pressure that I felt was enormous.

Carlos: So you talked about business school. You actually didn't go to undergrad, is that correct? You didn't get a Bachelor's degree?

Sean McDermott: *No. I have no college experience.*

Carlos: But you went to business school and that's where we met. In the executive MBA program at Temple. Do you think that it just added to your pedigree for the times that fancy titles, and pieces of paper matter to people? Or do you think it actually added to your experience as an entrepreneur, as a business owner, and made it better?

Sean McDermott: *My experience at business school, at Fox Business School. I had a very good experience.*

entrepreneurs

Everything that I had learned to that point was self-taught. I learned to write a return, to figure out the net present value of a project. I learned how to negotiate. I learned how to do these things just by reading books. And then and not just reading one book but reading another book. And not just reading those books but actually creating a plan, and taking action to go forward, and to implement this stuff.

One thing business school taught me; I know now how to put formal names to processes. I didn't know what continuous improvement was. We constantly want to improve. Oh, I didn't know it was called Kaizen. Now I do. So now I'm really smart.

I remember our operations class they were talking about the continuous improvement. Kaizen. We do it all the time. We try to look at a process and ask, "how do we make this better?"

And then someone says, "well, why don't we try this?"

And then it's, "why?"

Or, "that's good, why don't we try this too."

And we put these ideas together and try and narrate them and try and get a better process. But that was probably the funnier part of our operations course. Like, all right, I do this already.

And he asks, "you do this already?"

I say, "I do that already but we call it this."

He's like, "oh, no, they, they call it this."

Okay, whatever. I'm the type of guy if you want to take something very complicated; I need it really dumbed down. I need to understand from a dumbed down way of looking at it, in order to make sense of it, to bring it forward,

entrepreneurs

so I can see not just what it is, but why it matters, and how i can utilize is to my advantage.

So business school was great for me because I met people like you. I met the people in my group who will be with me the rest of my life. What I got out of business school isn't what I thought I was going to get. And what I thought I was going to get was something higher than what I already knew. And what I realized is, I learned everything I needed to learn by just reading those books. By paying attention, by asking the right questions to other entrepreneurs and private investors. Business school gave me access to a network of people with unique advice. It gave me a great shared experience. But I would say if anyone is going to business school and they're entrepreneurial already, and they think they're going to get a better business acumen, they're probably wrong.

I'm glad I went there. I'm glad I met the people who I met. I know have a degree and I did it in a very unorthodox way. And I'm going to go get another degree. I'm going to do that, the dual Master's Degree in Innovation and Strategy. And the reason I'm going to do that is, now it's more about my kids. I wanna show my girls that there's, nothing in this world that people can tell you, you can't do.

When I first started my business, when I would ask people for advice, I should of asked for experience from people instead. But I asked for, "what do you think?" I don't know why I was asking some of these people what they thought because I didn't really care what they thought. And none of them had any confidence in me anyway, except for one guy.

entrepreneurs

One guy said, "I think whatever you do you're going to be extraordinarily successful at it."

Everyone else said things like, "what do you know about business? You're going to get killed. You have no idea what you're doing."

And my answer for all that internally was, I do know I don't need that negativity. I think that I know something that they don't. And that gap is what creates the doubt in their minds. By far I'm not a Zuckerberg. I'm not sure I really aspire to be that type of person. Because I'm not sure they even run their businesses anymore. I like being an entrepreneur. Jeff Bezos, and Zuckerberg, and Sara Blakely, they are more in the public eye at this point. They're making decisions and giving input in their business but they have some extremely intelligent people working with them. And that's not to take any credit away from them. They're obviously brilliant men, and brilliant women who are entrepreneurs, who are at that status.

I believe that when looking at someone that big, they're technically not running the business anymore. Their businesses are set up. They're running with or without them. What they need to be is to be a visionary. To figure out the next thing to do. Facebook is X today but what's it going to be tomorrow? Is it Y or Z? How are they going to reinvent themselves. Amazon is doing it. Every day it seems like Amazon comes out with something different. Every time I read about Amazon they're trying something new. And they're just an amazing company to be able to do that.

The one thing I think that ties all entrepreneurs together is that they have this clear vision. That they're going to be successful. That nothing will get in the way. I

entrepreneurs

think that's vision, the vision of where someone's wants to go is a huge driving force. It might sound crazy to some people and a lot of times it does. But when you get a few people to follow that vision, it becomes contagious. That's what I think.

I also know that some of the people who you start a business with in the beginning, I mean in employee wise, they're not going to make it. May not make it. As you going from phase one to 10. Because they miss that startup period. They like that. They like that you come to them for advice or opinions or whatever. Now all of a sudden you have another person bolted on to you and that's very challenging and their role may be diminished and they feel infective now, although they're doing an excellent job.

And these are things that no one ever talks about in entrepreneurship. People disappear and people who thought had a big role to play in the company and they still do, but in their eyes they don't anymore because the company is growing.

I've heard someone say to me, "you've become too corporate."

I'm the farthest thing from corporate.

Carlos: So how do you deal with that? Because that's almost on a personal level, right? It's no longer; the business isn't worth it, or something business related. Where they need to make more money or they want more responsibility. At that point how do you separate those personal feelings? I feel like Jeff Bezos doesn't know all 500,000 employees at Amazon, right? That's impossible, it's not even natural.

entrepreneurs

But because you have a small business, and when you have 10 people and then one person leaves, that's 10% of your workforce. You've probably known that person and worked with them for quite a while. You've developed more than just a professional relationship. At that point, you get along with them; you've built a friendship, right? So that line between professionalism and personal starts to blur. How do you manage that? How do you manage those feelings as a human being, as we all are?

Sean McDermott: *So everyone who works for me I care about. And I would hope that if this company went to 100 million dollars, I'd have the same affection for everyone who worked there. I'd wanna know who those people are. Wealth is not my end goal. I think wealth will happen by doing a good job. Wealth is a symptom of doing a good job. Running a successful company, wealth comes with that. My goal is to create things. But how do I manage those people or how do I manage those feelings? I just treat people like I'm a part of their team. They look at me maybe as their leader or whatever. But I look at them and I need them as much as they need me. It's reciprocal. It isn't all on me. It isn't all on them. If people leave I'm screwed. That's the truth.*

If Amazon has 10% of their people quit that's not a roadblock, right? They've probably got 100,000 applicants waiting to get in there. I don't. I don't have that resource to tap. So I treat everyone fairly. I treat everyone with respect. I care about people who work for me. When things are happening in people's lives, I want to know about it. An employee just had a baby and we made sure that we sent

entrepreneurs

a nice gift basket to her house. That's something that I would continue if we got to $50 million dollars or a $150 million dollars.

To me that's personal. That's caring about people. That's showing you're not a robot, sitting behind a desk, just demanding orders and pounding on the table and smoking cigars. There's more to it than that. I care what happens to people when they go home. On the weekends. How did they live their lives? I don't try to be intrusive or caddish but they do share things with me. But you know people get married, people get divorced, they have kids. And some things should be celebrated.

We make sure that, it's probably something really stupid but we send out these stupid E-cards. From American? I think it's like American Signature. To everyone who works for us on their birthday. How many people do that? How many employers remember when the people who work for them, when their birthdays are? And we send some personalized card to them that's funny and goofy.

And everyone says, "that made my day." That someone else besides your family remembered who you are. And you're talking about 40 something year old men and women, 30 something year old people. And like I said, we send stuff for people who are celebrating new births and extending their family. And I feel it's an extension of our team, our family.

I remember a woman came to me and said, "this guy should be laid off."

And I said, "Why?"

"Because of A, B, C, and D."

I said, "so, what's the solution?"

entrepreneurs

"Lay him off. Get rid of him"
I said, "that's not the solution. What's the solution?" Tell me what it is. If you're going to bring me a problem, bring me a solution too. I said, "The solution is more training, we need to get him more training." Because that individual has a personality, and is a great human being and you can build a business unit around him.

Carlos: What do you think is tougher? You talk a lot about leadership, so do you think it's tougher to lead your employees? Or manage the business? Which side provides the most stress in your life?

Sean McDermott: *Probably the management side. The leadership side to me, comes easy. On the way down was talking to one of my guys and fleshing out ideas. Fleshing out problems that, maybe they may see them as problems on the surface. And I'm trying to get them to look past that. Like, yeah it's a problem you see this. You see this car accident or whatever. But what you don't see is maybe something good can come out of it.*

They need to be thinking strategically of where the company is going. They need to be thinking, who are the right people to put there. You know. Who would make the right team people that will deliver what we're trying to do and get to the end. And not putting the wrong people on the bus.

Leadership is an individual, what's the technical term? An individual who's leading a group of individuals for a common goal. Or a shared vision. Where management doesn't have that. To be a manager you need to have certain tools to get tasks done. A manager's job is to make

entrepreneurs

sure that people are getting the work done. That is the managing processes.

Relationships, that's hard. That's hard and it's because people I think can be inherently distrustful. I also think a lot of people in manager positions are actually not managers. They've just been given that role because they've been there for 10 years. It's almost like, you think you're going to quit and then nope, we're going to make you a manager. And all of a sudden this person who hated their job now became a manager and now really hates their job. And they should have just left. But they're going to stay there and, realistically that's why I think that's why people hate managers because they torture other people. Because they hate their job because they didn't really want to be there.

And if you ask a bad manager how to do a capital budget, they probably will have no idea even what you're talking about. Going outside of your comfort zone a little bit, makes you become a better person, and sometimes you have to force yourself to do that. Deal with a tough situation. I think leadership has something to do with that also. But if you're looking at the leadership team up top, they need to be setting where the team is going. And the managers need to be driving down that road with the people. That's how I look at it. Managers need are executing, we are turning left, we are turning right. That's how I look at the difference.

I think I said manager is a tougher position but now I'm thinking leadership is a lot harder. I don't know if that makes sense. Because without the vision and without the

entrepreneurs

strategic vision you'll never get there. And you won't need the manager.

It's like the chicken for the egg or, right? As a leader you're going to think differently. You're going to think bigger and then you build your management structures. I think leadership is really important and I think people define leadership differently. People throw that word around and I don't think they actually know what it means. I think they believe that leadership is being an asshole.

They think, "I'm the leader of this company because I bought 20% interest."

No, you're an assigned leader. You didn't earn the position. You got that title because you had the money to pay for it. That doesn't mean you are qualified to lead anyone. And that doesn't mean anyone around here wants to be led by you. And that's the difference.

I think I'm going to say something that probably most people would disagree with but I don't think leaders are taught. I don't think you can learn to become a leader. I think if you're a leader, leadership knowledge will make you a better leader. I think if you're not a leader and you don't have the right personality to lead, you will fight every piece of that. Where someone who may have maybe that creative mindset, versus an analytical mindset because I think that's more of an engineer, who is able to see the big picture, who can think big, or a person that has something that allows them to do those things, can be a leader. Or if they are able to get out of their comfort zone. I feel like those are the people running the companies properly.

And I think when, back to what you led with, talking about small businesses, and then maybe look at the reason

entrepreneurs

why small businesses fail. I mean, I'm going to say directly it's because of the leadership. Because if you have the correct leadership you're going to want to understand your financial numbers. You're going to want to understand how to get a better employee. You're going to wanna understand how to do X, Y and Z better than your competition.

So when I think about people who start ventures, sometimes these are people who are in a closet by themselves with no windows, limited oxygen and they're not leaders. And then they start a company and they think that they can lead a crew. And no one wants to follow them and then their companies just crash and burn.

Carlos: Maybe it's a chicken or egg argument. Maybe it changes, or can change from one situation to another. Maybe it depends on how your day is going. I think how you manage will impact how you lead and how you lead will impact how you manage. Maybe it wasn't a fair question.

But since we're talking about leadership and management let's talk about having employees. Because having employees means you need both to be competent at both. So what's the biggest challenge for you, having employees?

Sean McDermott: *Managing the different personalities that people have. Getting people to understand why you're changing, why you're doing this. Every company is changing. If you're not changing you're dying. It's not acceptable to do what we did three months ago, we're not doing that anymore we're doing this. And having a clear concise message for them so they understand. So they're coming along with you. That's how I feel. They need to see*

entrepreneurs

why you're doing it, and one-on-one I think they get exactly what we're doing and why we're doing it. Because they've seen the growth. And they're the good employees.

The bad employees are people who think that they're smarter than everyone. And they might be. They might be smarter than me. But they should go and work for someone else. They should become competition. A lot of people think that they have all the answers and they're the people you should be weary of. And we've had some employees in the past who feel like that. And what they don't realize is, no one is listening to them. As soon as they start talking, people shut down. Although they might be right, they feel they're smarter than everyone else and they're going to show you how smart they are. They might be right. They might be, they very well might be. But it's the delivery, it's how they say it. It's like the person who knows everything. Do you wanna be around that person? I wanna be the dumbest guy in the room. I wanna be a sponge. If you're the guy always talking about how smart you are, who the hell wants to be around that guy right? You run away, I run away from those people.

There was an individual who worked here who couldn't wait to tell people why they were wrong. It might sound cliché but getting those people off the bus before they ruin things can make a world of difference. When you realize that no one can build anything around them. They're just not a good person. People don't like them. When they're talking, people are trying to do anything they can do to get away from them to the point where if they could, they would jump off a cliff. That's when you know they're a bad employee.

entrepreneurs

People who I'm around who have similar personalities to me, who think a lot like me. I don't mean people who think the same things as me. It's more about how they think. How are they interacting with others, and I like people who want to learn, who want to listen, those are the people I'm attracted to. And there are people I like less maybe. People who think they know everything, I repel them. I want to stay away from them. Where some people are trying to figure that type of person out, I don't need to figure that out. I just know that they're not where I want to be in life. People that aren't open to learning are not people who I wanna connect with. And actually I feel like they recognize that also. They don't wanna connect with me because they know I'm going to call their BS. Or ignore them and that might kill them too. Because they need that attention, they need that affection. They need that reassurance that what they're saying is the right thing.

But managing good employees is great. Managing bad employees, that's a whole different story. How to get good employees? You've got to do your due diligence. What's the saying, if you listen to yourself you have a fool for a client. That's me. So when I bring in people to be interviewed, I don't just interview them myself, I have someone else interview them as well. If they don't have referrals, things like that, that's a red flag. When I look at someone's resume, and there's other key things like they're applying for a mechanics job but they've only worked at Dairy Queen. Obviously we can't even have a discussion, right? So people get an interview if I look at their resume and there are not gaps in it, they have references, they have some experience.

entrepreneurs

And then we grade them and Trish will ask some questions and I'll ask some questions or Ray will ask some questions and we grade them. If it's Ray or Trish or someone else, they get to ask any question they like. It's formalized but I don't tell people what questions they should ask. I say here's the resume. Take a look at it and tell me what you think. But I'm grading what? I'm grading the question, the individual, and the answers we're getting. On a scale of one to 10. Because we wanna hear the question, we wanna hear the answer from these people. But it's a formalized process.

Once they get to that point in their interview we document it. We take an average of the number, they either get another interview or not. We talk about why, what would make that person a good employee here? Would they take synergies away from what we've already created or would they add to it? Are they bringing value? And that's, I think that's the real key thing. Is there value being brought?

If they don't hit seven and a half on an average, between at two or three of us they don't get another interview. And these are not even questions about the trade. These are about being a human being. This is about the type of person sitting in front of me is. Is this someone that's going to steal from me? If they're going to steal from me, they're going to steal from our customers. But I want to know things about them. So I might ask them what do they read. These are maybe unorthodox questions but I want to know what you read. I want to know what you do in your free time. I want to know like how you treat other people. There's a key question that I ask; if I ask you to do something illegal that would have a positive effect, would

entrepreneurs

you do it? How many people do you think would say I would never do that?

Carlos: Probably fewer than I would guess. My automatic instinct is like, I'm not going to jail for you. I would like a paycheck but I can't go to jail for you.

Sean McDermott: *You're not even working for me. That's the funny part. That's the reason I ask these questions. And a lot of times we'll extend the interview once they say they would. And at that point I'm like alright, well; tell me what you do for fun? Now we're just having a conversation. The interview is over.*

Carlos: There are two main strategies for hiring that different companies, and this goes for large or small, a lot of companies will see an amazing resume, with a very wonderful pedigree. The candidate went to all the right schools, and they have all the right experience; but they don't really ask them who they are; what they like to do; how they treat their mother. They're so excited. This guy's so qualified; we're going to bring him on. Or she's super smart; she has all the skills that we need. Versus, who is this person? Are they a good fit for the role and for the company? Will they mesh well with the team?

When I hire I'm concerned about the technical side. A good candidate definitely needs the basic skills I'm looking for but I can work with them. I am confident I can train a person in areas they might not be as strong in. That's the easy part. The more difficult task, and the areas I'm more concerned with who they're going to be. Are they going to work well with us? Is it going to be a good fit for everyone? Are they going to be happy? If I hire someone

entrepreneurs

who is just going to be miserable doing the day to day tasks what good did I do them, or myself, or the company?

But it sounds like you're focused more on the personal side, the emotional intelligence. Are they going to steal from me? Can I trust them? Can I put them in front of a customer? How did you come to that decision? When did you learn that aspect of human resources? Because I think that's what a lot of people struggle with. How do you balance those needs? Do I have to hire someone who has experience versus; I need to hire someone that's going to work well with the company, right? Because most often, I've found, it becomes a tradeoff. We're all human so nobody will ever be perfect.

Sean McDermott: *Right, that's a good question too. That's what happens, that's really what it comes down to. But all of that just comes from experiencing bad employees, bad hires and why. And so I started really thinking I have to change this process up. This is not working. If a guy is here for three months and he leaves, that costs me probably $20,000. Right off my bottom line. A bad employee is going to hit you on net profit. Because you still need someone. Once they go, you gotta get someone back in there. That's what makes it hard.*

But it was all just a learning experience from hiring bad people. Making mistakes and learning from those mistakes. I started off hiring people because they pass the mirror test. Can they fog up a mirror? If they can fog up a mirror, they got a job. And I was just asking bullshit questions. Like hey yeah, how do you know this guy? It was bullshit. And I needed to be more formalized when doing interviews because I didn't have a process. And the

entrepreneurs

people who are giving recommendations for someone, they need to understand that they're working for a legitimate company and we're not just giving out paychecks as a charity. And my team gets it now. I think before they just wanted to help someone out and say yeah, let's bring them on. But now they know that if a new guy can't pass me, my guys in the field will spit them out. And when that happens they won't say it direct. They won't come out and say I won't work with that guy. What usually ends up happening is I'll say hey, do you want to work with X?

And they go, "no, I'll do it myself."

Then I know I have a problem. I need to know why. I need to know what happened; why that happened; and then when I talk to the guys one-on-one they'll let me know. And they should let me know because to me this is important, this is their company too. They need to be comfortable communicating, and they need to be happy.

For example we had an individual here who was an, angry, angry person unfortunately. Nice guy, technically smart, had a career in front of him that he basically flushed down the toilet. But he couldn't control his emotions. What I said to him when I questioned him was that I was concerned they were going to go nuts on one of my customers.

And he said, "I would never do that."

And quickly I realized well what you just told me is you can control your emotions. You're also telling me you're choosing not to. So if you're getting upset with mechanics or other people on your team there's only one step: you're going to go nuts on one of my customers eventually because you're going to choose not to control that emotion. And of

entrepreneurs

course when you challenge someone they sit there and they deny that would ever, ever, ever happen. And then sure enough three months, six months later it's exactly what happens.

So at that point I'm thinking I'm going to mitigate my loss now and get rid of this guy. And that sounds like such a cold thing but I have other people working in this company that I need to be concerned with and worried about. And that this individual has basically set aside how everyone else should be treated. People shouldn't be thinking fuck I have to work with this guy tomorrow. And they shouldn't be on their drive to work like how's this guy going to be today?

That's not a good environment to work in. It becomes very toxic. And eventually other employees will leave to get away from that. And by talking to your people and just asking key questions you'll figure that out.

It's just like getting in front of customers and asking how everything is. You know when we're doing sales I ask key questions. The customers will figure out if they have a bad contractor. Just because I'm in front of them doesn't mean they want to change contractors. They might just need me for a number. But if they have a bad contractor, like I have a bad employee, they'll do the same. They'll have the same reaction.

If I ask them, um, "who you dealing with right now, you know who's your contractor?"

And they go, "we're dealing with ABC Industries."

And I'm like, "oh good, I heard about them, they're a pretty good contractor, are you happy with them?"

entrepreneurs

They're going to do one of two things, just like I would do with an employee, maybe not to other employees. But their body language is going to give them away.

They go, "uh..." or they're going to say, "well, they're okay, but..."

Or they're going to say they're great. And at that point, I'm like why am I here? And it's the same thing with employees. When you hear about good employees you want to know why. So either way I'm asking questions. Well what's so great about that contractor? Tell me about them, I wanna hear about them. Why is ABC Industries such a great contractor? And they'll tell me, I'm thinking, that's my competition, thank you for giving me a little education.

But it's the same thing with a good employee. I brag about the guys we have here never wanting to leave. They do an incredible job. I feel like they all see what we're trying to do here. But managing employees and making that change, realizing we need to have a better process of how to hire people was all learned through trial and error. But constantly improving that process and improving how we hire is important because that's our initial step into how we're going to write the culture we want into this company and keep it here and maintain it. It's through each employee.

Carlos: Now that you've refined your hiring process and you've got all the right team members who understand, who are engaged, who want to learn how do you manage retention at that point? I feel like a lot of times when you have these star players, they're not going to be content to just collect a paycheck. That's part of the reason you're hiring them. It's because they do have that something

entrepreneurs

extra. They have that personality you're looking for. So how do you manage continued growth, and continued engagement, for employees in your business?

Sean McDermott: *The fact that they know that we're growing, is one thing. Having a culture of learning, is another one of the things that would be stressed. Emphasize training. We send techs, and my techs are unionized, and there is union training that they can get. And then there's other training that they can get that's specialized. And there are people who feed off that. They love it, and I love it. I love the fact that they're really interested in making themselves a better human being.*

So I think the fact that we like seeing that type of training and investing in them. I think the fact that they're not employee 4219, you know? They're John Smith. We know who these people are. We care about who they are. We write newsletters about them. Well I write a newsletter every month and I highlight someone in there or a group of people like the apprentices or the people working at this site. But I constantly reaffirm my appreciation for them and how great they are.

Could they get that somewhere else? Maybe. I'm guessing they could. But I think the fact that they can call me and talk to me. And I can relate to them and know we can solve a problem together. I just treat people with respect and I think that's really what it comes down to.

There's a lot of things that we've read in business books that come down to you know there's this scale or this ladder. And there's some industries where there is a ladder to really climb. And in this industry there's not. I mean I could start hiring internally and I'm very well going to as

entrepreneurs

guys get older and get a little bit beat up. I don't want them to quit. I don't want them to go work at a hospital or something to do bare minimum. They have the skillset so why wouldn't we keep them? They can be salespeople. A set of eyes to help sell what they know.

But I took, well god, maybe it was like, time flies, so it could have been a little over two years ago, where I went around to every guy. We went out to lunch or something and I would ask them a bunch of different questions. Anywhere from what type of music you listen to; what do you listen to right now; in your iPad or iPod or iPhone or Android or whatever. What's your favorite cheesesteak place in Philadelphia? Where do you see yourself in five years? You know, they all say the same thing, Precision Mechanical. But that's not the reality sometimes because people leave.

But I did that because I want to know what they really want. Because there are things that people do and then there are things that people like to do. And I wanna know what they like to do because if we can marry those two things together, why wouldn't we? You know there are certain people through the years who have talked about maybe starting their own company.

And I say, and I always say come to me first and I'll help you. I know I can help you or maybe I can be a part of that with you. But I am more than willing to help. Why would I let talent just escape? Fly away. They can leave if they like but I don't want them to. So if they're going to leave because they're going to start a business, make me your partner. I can help you. There are things that I've done,

entrepreneurs

things that I've made mistakes with, and you don't have to repeat those same mistakes, and I can make things easier.

And maybe that's another reason why people want to work here. And they want work for me, and they want to work for Ray. Because I don't have any sort of arrogance or pretentiousness about who I am or what I've done. I can help people follow that path; I would love to do that with them.

Carlos: Yeah. It really says a lot about who you are as a person. That level of really commitment to your employees. To your family as you put it. About family you said you have three kids. How does running your business, uh, impact your personal and family life?

Sean McDermott: *I have three kids. They are four, going to be three, and 11 months. And as I can, where I can, I stay home a little bit longer to have breakfast with them. I make sure every night I read stories to them. I make sure that if they need me I am there. And that includes my wife. Because the good thing about being an entrepreneur is that I can start at 2 o'clock in the morning. If I need to get that contract out, I don't need to get up at 7:00am and start working, I can get up at 2:00 in the morning and I can start working.*

So family, to me, is extremely important. One of the reasons why I did everything with going through the MBA was to show my girls that you can do anything. Right? There are no roadblocks in life that people can put in front of you verbally or whatever. There are ways to do anything. But I try to spend as much time as I can with my family. We go for walks. There are horses on the path we take, and we check out the horses.

entrepreneurs

I try to make sure that my relationship with my kids is different than my relationship with how my dad was. My dad was constantly working. We had five kids in the family, and he wasn't always there. And not because he didn't want to be there, because he was working and trying to make sure that we were fed. We had school to go to, and all those things. But I'm trying to make sure there's a little difference there being more physically present.

So one of the things I try to do and I'm going to try to do more is start bringing my kids to entrepreneurial events. Like once a year starting next year we're going to go to this entrepreneurial connection event and I'm going to bring all my kids and my wife. We did it when my Milly was just a baby. She's going to be three. Addy was just a little over two. And it was great to share that experience with them. But when my kids get old enough to start remembering those things, I want them to feel those experiences and see the processes. And think that you don't have to work for someone if you don't want to. If you have an idea, bring it forward. That's how I look at it.

Carlos: So you talked early on about sobriety. I grew up my dad was a heroin addict. He stopped when my mom got pregnant with my sister. But he kept drinking and when I was three, he decided to get sober. So from basically from the age of about three and a half, until I was maybe 13 or 14, I went to weekly AA meetings. I've been to more AA meetings than most people will ever go to in their life. Even once they've recovered. Because a lot of times you get to recovery you start going from weekly to monthly, to semi-annual and then you show up annually once in a while.

entrepreneurs

But I wanted to talk about this because I think a lot of times people hear you own your own business they get this preconceived notion about who you are. And they'll think oh, you're a business owner, you must have everything going for you. You're doing everything right.

Particularly as a successful business owner people might be prone to say or think you're doing everything right, this guy is so great.

I think people overlook the flawed side of a person's humanity. The side where everyone falls, everyone trips, everyone stumbles. I think the difference between someone who is successful and someone who continues to stumble is that a successful person decides to make a change.

So I was just curious how addiction impacted you. How it impacts you on a day-to-day basis? How it has shaped the way you view your business? You talked a little bit about the way you see things is completely different. Do you talk about that part of your life that with your employees? Do you think you treat your employees differently as a result of your experience?

Sean McDermott: *I think. Well sobriety is massive in my life because if I drank, all this would disappear. It would explode because I wouldn't be here. When I got sober probably a month after the fact, I kind of just realized that when I was drinking I was very lonely. When you get sober, you have all these people around you who want to help and they're happy for you.*

Getting sober really opened up the doors for me to recognize my potential and to capitalize on it. And when I say capitalize on it, just at least taking that initial step.

entrepreneurs

Thinking well, I know how bad it could be. How bad could it be if I just try to do something that can be successful? Instead of thinking well I know if I do this then I know where I'm going to go. It's kind of like; maybe mentally playing out a tape in your mind of what could happen and what could not. And if I drink beer or whiskey or whatever, what's going to happen to me tonight; or tomorrow? Would I go to work tomorrow? Would I go to work for the next month? Would I cheat on my wife? These are the things that'll happen; these are the things I know will happen to me, because of me, if I drink.

There's something that happens to me when I put alcohol in my body just like there's something that happens to people when they put sugar in their body. They can't stop eating or something. When I put alcohol in my body, I become an animal. And probably the best way to put it is, Doctor Jekyll and Mr. Hyde. I become unrecognizable to other people, and to myself. And when I look in the mirror I don't know who I am. I remember looking into that mirror at some point in my life asking myself who is that person? I just looked crazy. And the reality is: I was. I was losing my mind.

When you drink every day, you're pouring it, to press something bad in your body, yeah; bad things are going to happen. That's just cause and effect. So, the opposite is when you remove it, that bad thing, what happens? Good things happen in your life. And I think when you're abusing alcohol, or someone is an addict, they tend to think they don't deserve that. And I think people need to give themselves a break and love themselves and think understand that they do deserve that.

entrepreneurs

I should be able to recognize that and think hey, well, life is pretty good. You know and it might not be good tomorrow but today it is and I need to recognize that. And a lot of that bled into the business. A lot of that turned into treating people with respect; into being humble. I'm not saying I was that way when I started the company, all the way till now. But I learned and got better at it. But chances are in 10 years I'll feel the same exact way.

But getting sober, and this is going to sound really odd, getting sober is the worst thing that could ever happen in your life if you're drinking. It's the worst, actually the worst. And so if you're a person who likes to drink or likes to do drugs and you decide to go to AA that is the first feeling that's going to happen. And now you are in a position in life, where you have to decide to stay sober or decide to go back and to drink.

Carlos: So much of your identity is tied to drinking. It's extremely social for a lot of people even just being around alcohol.

Sean McDermott: *Absolutely. And now people go man, you must be really screwed up. Because you actually stopped doing this activity and went to AA to go drink coffee or whatever and listen to different people's experiences and share their experiences. But if you decide to stay sober, you're going to get the nice things in life. Not from things given to you but you will have a job; you'll build relationships; you'll accomplish goals. It's a lot easier to find success when you're not drunk. And people are going to trust you. If you go back out and drink or do drugs all of that new found success will be destroyed because now you*

entrepreneurs

have knowledge in your mind that you never had before, and all of that is going to fade away again.

12 steps for example, that idea has got nothing to do with going to AA. It talks about giving yourself up to a higher power. I use the meeting rooms as my higher power, the people, and the fellowship that is in there. But if you look at AA or NA and just going to meetings there's nothing to that about being a good human being.

That's why the 12 steps are important, just so important. I make sure if I offended anyone or hurt people's feelings, I tell them that day, I'm sorry. And that's a humbling thing to do; to admit that you did something wrong. If I have resentments towards someone, towards my family, if it's fears, I talk about that. It lets people who can actually help me flesh that stuff out or identify, maybe a crack in my thinking. You know if you hurt someone, apologize. If you have resentments, I talk about them. If things are holding you back you should talk about that. You want to talk to a therapist or you wanna talk to a friend about it. But if you think that you're just going to talk about it and things are going to get well, that doesn't always happen you have to do work.

And all this goes back into business. This is exactly the format of thinking going into business, while you're in business. If you did something wrong in the business, admit it. Fall on the sword and tell the customer it was a mistake what I did there. Forgive me. It won't happen again, I promise it won't happen again. And not just that if they give you that chance, follow through on that promise. These are the things my experience with sobriety that I

entrepreneurs

have meshed with my business. Things like talking about your mistakes and owning up to them.

Communicating right? If you have a fear about something in your business, talk about it. Who can you talk to about that stuff? Talk to another entrepreneur. They probably know what you're going through, they lived through it. They've done it. They've probably thought whatever you're thinking right now. And they've probably already thought about it a lot longer.

Respect the people who are around you, from your employees, to your family. Think about how special they are. If you're abusing drinking or abusing drugs there, there is no retirement. You're going to die or go to jail, that's it. That's it. Your family is going to hate your guts. No one is going to wanna be around you. No one wants to be around people who are selfish. Nobody likes people who are extremely selfish. Be the opposite way of that. Be how, I mean how I think of it is that I love myself and that I want to treat people, or I want to give people that same love. But when you're a selfish human being, where you're stealing from people you love, who wants to be around that individual? And if you do want to be around someone like that, maybe there's something wrong with you.

Carlos: It kind of seems dysfunctional. Maybe it works. I don't know, but it seems dysfunctional. That type of relationship where someone is abusing you. But you've been doing this for 10 years now both sobriety and your company. I'm sure there have been ups and downs. Was there ever a point where you're just like alright, I'm out. I'm done; I have to do something else.

entrepreneurs

Sean McDermott: *Never. Best decision I ever made. That's how I look at it. But I had a parachute. Do you just jump off and nosedive or do you jump off and think okay I have a parachute and I have a backup too. The backup was: there is no going back to work. But as someone who's wants to be an entrepreneur, realistically they're not going to ever take that nosedive because really that entrepreneurship is the controlled jump off a cliff. An entrepreneur will always think I'm not coming back. This is it. I know I'm going to land eventually; it's just how hard am I going to land? Is that cliff two feet or is it 200 feet? Or maybe it's not a cliff at all.*

Am I going to die? Or am I going to be okay; am I going to just roll? Now did doubt ever occur in my mind? Yeah of course it did. I'm going to say doubt creeps in my mind for maybe three minutes and I squash it. I'm start to realize this is just my alcoholic brain thinking; telling me that I'm not good enough to do this crap. And I just start thinking fuck that. I'm going to crush it. I'm not listening to that nonsense. That's just self-pity bullshit.

Carlos: Do you ever feel like you're successful? That you've achieved your goals?

Sean McDermott: *I'll say that I've come far enough to know that if I'm not going to be 100 million dollar business that's okay. My family is going to be okay, I'm going to be okay. There's not a number out there that would make me feel more successful.*

There was a book that I was reading. <u>Start With Why</u>, by Simon Sinek. And at the end he talks about this whole Birthing of Giants. I actually got accepted to this program. I'm going to be going next year. It's somewhere

entrepreneurs

down in Duke? But at some point that Birthing of Giants was affiliated with the Entrepreneur's Organization.

And it was at the MIT Endicott House. And it was in a room, I'm hoping I got this right. It was in this room and the guy who was leading the presentation asked, and it's like, September or something and he asked how many people in this room have hit their numbers for the year? And boom 80% of hands go up. Then he asked the question how many people in this room feel successful? And no hands went up. So how do you feel successful?

So I feel that way. I don't feel successful. Like I'm no different than I was when I started the business till now. I don't feel successful. Sometimes I think if I start to feel successful I'm becoming arrogant. Like I'm pretentious; or like someone has been lying to me. That's the best way to put it; the idea that you're not that special. And that's how I try to always keep myself grounded. And that question is something that I always keep in the back of my mind. How do I feel successful? I feel accomplished in some things in life.

There's a great, great, soccer coach and it's my favorite soccer team, Manchester United. And there was this guy Alex Ferguson, who was the coach. And, I saw him speak at the Kimmel Center, me and my wife. My wife knows I love Manchester United. I've been following them since I was 10 years old. But he's a retired coach; he won like 26 titles in the premier league. Unheard of. Ridiculous. Probably the greatest manager in any sport ever. They're playing somewhere in the range of 60 some games a year. And this guy in 1999 won three of the biggest trophies in

entrepreneurs

the world. This guy was an unbelievable coach and he had an unbelievable team.

Just so you can see how great of a coach he was, the last year he coached they won the title. Then a coach took over the following year with the same exact team and they finished 6th where they ran away with it the year before. The guy is just a phenomenal coach. My point in saying this is when they won the titles, and the reporters are there and they're asking him how he felt the next day, how he felt. And he said something like I celebrated and I was extremely happy. I'm not quoting him correctly but he said something along the lines that he felt happy. He felt a sense of accomplishment. And when he woke up the next day he was planning for the next thing. That was over. That happened already and it's over with. He experienced it. He felt it. He moved on. That's exactly how I feel. When I have a big win I think great how do I keep that? How do I keep that momentum going? How do I take what we did today, roll it up in a ball, package it, either the same exact way or even better and hand it off to someone else.

And that's I think that's key. I know people who are entrepreneurs and they live in huge, huge houses. I'm not going to say they live above their means or anything like that. But they might have a lot of debt. And they're driving a ridiculous car and they go on vacations for like three months out of the year. How does that look on the outside? Does that look pretentious in a way? To the people who are working for you? When you're that type of person?

I saw a guy he was renting a jet and he was saying he's living the entrepreneur life. He was living the "rock star" life. And I'm thinking but you're making probably $20

entrepreneurs

million a year. Why would you say that? Like what gives? What kind of arrogance is oozing out of you that would make you want to feel and say that. And alienate the people who are actually helping you live that lifestyle. You were talking about emotional intelligence. Being aware of who you are. Is that really awareness? Is that how your mother raised you? That's really what it comes down to. Maybe some mothers did I don't know. But I know my mom didn't. I try to be a little bit more humble about things because my employees are watching me.

And really it's in creating things that gives me more joy than the money that follows behind it. If your mindset is just that you're going to make a lot of money here you better figure out how you're going to do that. You better work backwards to figure that out. You better pick a number and work backwards. And figure out how big does your business gotta be to make X amount of dollars a year. And if you can't do that, you shouldn't be in business.

I had a guy tell me that he wanted to make $400,000 a year. And I asked him how he was going to do that. He had no accounts, no plans, no ideas other than he wanted to make money. That's what I'm going to make he said. Okay I'm not against that but how are you going to do that? You gotta work backwards. Your job is then to figure out what your revenue needs to be to earn that much. You're managing and you're looking at your cost of goods. And you're looking at your operating expenses. It all comes out of how much you can compensate yourself. About how much you can pull out of the business. So how well did you manage that? And that compensation becomes a direct result of running a good business. If you run a good

entrepreneurs

business you'll make money. Once again good follows hard work. It's like a wave. That's how I look at it. There are ups and downs and sometimes things are not always good

Just like when 2008 happened and we were in business and we had people call us up and tell us that whatever we were doing put our tools down. They had no money to pay us. The only reason why we survived is because we had service contracts signed. But there were not a lot of businesses that survived during that time. Somehow we didn't have to layoff anyone. The entire time I was thinking if we can get through this, we'll get through anything. And I think it's true. It was a difficult time. But no one got laid off and somehow or another, we managed some kind of growth that year. I can't tell you how. Luck; that's really what it came down to because you can't plan for those types of waves.

Carlos: What has your biggest success so far with your business? You don't like that word. So what's been your biggest accomplishment? Of all the goals you set, and they constantly change, but has there been one goal you reached and were like yeah, that felt good.

Sean McDermott: *I don't think I can narrow it down to one thing. Maybe our client base. Yeah I think just maintaining our client base. That's been it. I think it's maintaining the customers that we have. It makes me think if I can run this business with just these customers and they're extremely high-end customers, I can make it work with anyone.*

Yeah I really think that's what made us continue to grow. They've given us the opportunity to treat our employees even better than we hoped and our customers

entrepreneurs

benefit from that as well because we can provide great service.

Carlos: Other end of the spectrum now. What's been the biggest mistake you've made thus far; that one time where you just kind of think man I wish I could get that one back?

Sean McDermott: *I don't know if I'd say the only mistake that I made was a good mistake because I learned from them. But if there were any mistakes, probably in the beginning I wish I would have had a better plan about how to hire people. In the beginning it was basically, if they passed the mirror test. They had blood running through their veins so they got hired and maybe also with some sales people who we've hired. I don't know if I directly understood how a salesperson works, compared to how I work.*

And what the mindset of what success for a salesperson really looks like. Success to me is, you're getting customers, and you're getting retention. To sales, a success might be I talked to five people today. What's hot? What do you got? And I think I needed, even to this day, this is one of the harder things I need to learn is how to work with salespeople. Salespeople are critical to your business growing. Treating them the way they should be treated. We pull a lot of growth ourselves from our business and it comes in organically. But trying to manufacture that growth is a process with salespeople. And that's probably one thing I regret not having a better formalized plan for them.

entrepreneurs

Carlos: Do you ever make like hypothetical plans in case things go south? The economy tanks or you're just done and you wanna get out, or something else happens.

Sean McDermott: *No, I've never really thought of it that way. I always thought if the economy tanks the reality is there's nothing I can do to control that. That's the bottom of that wave. If there was something that I'm doing in a business, like if I was stealing from the business then that would be a major problem. Or my partner was stealing or something like that. Or an employee was stealing or something. I can actually control that if I catch it in time.*

But getting out of it? No. I do like this business. It is fun. The people who I deal with are very interesting, dynamic people. The mechanics we deal with are extremely intelligent, they're smart, and they're good human beings.

I don't know if I have any sort of; there is no fallback plan. You try to provide for your family but it's like you're in it. And I think most entrepreneurs will say when you're in it, you can become like a serial entrepreneur and start different businesses. And I think at that point then you're in 100%. If your business is running without you then maybe it's time to go and look at another business or taking your business to another level if you can do that.

But if there's other ways you can make some other investments where building on a complementary business to yours. God forbid if this one failed you would have like a fallback plan that was something within your industry, potentially. If it's selling equipment or if it's selling materials that are related to the business that you know are going to be commodities. That people are going to need. And maybe

entrepreneurs

specialize in it, something like that. That's something that I've thought about.

Carlos: So, you talked about you have a mentor that you speak with. Do you mentor anyone? Do you have anyone that you are mentoring?

Sean McDermott: *Yeah. I mean kind of. But it's going to be kind of something that relates to AA. So the people who have asked me to mentor them that comes down to the relationship. The reason why my mentor; I'm the mentee, he's the mentor, it works is because I drive it because he's busy. If I don't set the meetings up, if I'm not the one asking questions that challenge him, what's the point, right?*

So I have two mentors. Well I guess just one. Maybe I should say I have one. I haven't met with the other guy in a long time because my one mentor is basically filling the role. But the reason I met with him is because he does something not in the industry I am in. That was number one. He does something that is very unique that I don't understand. He has done and seen a lot and he has done things that I can only think about. He thinks big. But the reason I like that is because my thinking needs to change at times. He's going to challenge me on any bullshit that I bring up to him. He's not going to let me get away with it. Saying I want to do one thing and then he watches me implement the opposite, or not following through. He's going to hold me accountable. That's what the relationship is supposed to be. But first it needs to be someone that actually wants to be mentored. Because people love that word; mentor. They like saying that phrase; I want to be mentored.

entrepreneurs

So it's kind of like in AA, people want to be sponsored. Do people want to be sponsored; do you wanna get well in AA? Same thing in business, do you wanna get better? Do you wanna close your brain off and your mind to think that you know everything or do you wanna open it up? To the point where you realize you need to be a sponge. Your mentor is this human being who has graciously opened their life to you. They've opened their lives to you and opened up about things in their lives. They are willing to talk about things that they may not share with other people. About what they have done, mistakes they have made. And maybe if you're listening, you're not going to make those same mistakes.

But at the same time if you're asking them to be your mentor chances are you're thinking they're a high caliber human being. And their ethics are in line. They're morally right. They do the things and people follow them. They're every bit of a leader that you would want to be, plus.

So when people ask me to mentor them in business I kind of, I wanna ask them some questions to define what they mean by that. I need to get some clarification. I want to know what their expectation for what we're going to do. What do they want out of this? So I ask some simple things. And unfortunately the reality is people never have answers for those questions. They're really just looking for a friend. And I'm okay with that.

If you have a mentor or mentee relationship and it turns into a friendship, what's wrong with that, right? The problem with being a mentor is that most people don't like to be challenged. Most people don't like to hear that there's an opposing view of what their thinking is. Most people will

entrepreneurs

sure as shit just shut down. For example, I ask people questions to understand their financials. So if I ask some questions and they don't know I'm not trying to attack them. If they don't know that's okay we'll go through them. I'm not an accountant; I mean I just know what I know. If I asked you some questions, and you can't tell me, you shouldn't give me a bullshit answer. Just say, you don't know. And then we can find out together.

But I've never even gotten that far. So most recently, I'll give you this example; I met with a guy and he asked me to be his mentor. We were just having lunch and we were talking about stuff and he asked can you mentor me? Sure. I don't say no to anyone and especially when it's stuff like that.

You wanna go to lunch? You wanna talk about business? Let's do it. And you want me to help you flesh out some ideas? Let's do it. You want me to hold you accountable? I will. So I told him you need to drive it. Tell me when you want to meet. Or even better how about this; I'm going to set up the meeting right now. We're going to meet second Tuesday of each month or whatever. Or maybe we'll meet every other month or every quarter. And it's your job to pick the place, the time, all that good stuff.

So I give them all the parameters and give them complete control on how the relationship is going to develop. So then what happens? A week goes by, two weeks, and now 6 months later and I've never mentored anyway. I don't mentor anyone because that process never happened because a lot of people don't like the fact that they have to do work. That's probably the best way to put it. To me, my relationship with my mentor is massive because I don't

entrepreneurs

know how much it would cost to go out and pay for it. That's really what it comes down to. To me it's worth a lot. If he said to me it's going to cost you $12,000 a year and you can have four hours a month for my time I think I would do it. It's that valuable to me. What I get from him, I can't get from any professor. He's a practitioner, he's doing it. He's the guy who creates wealth for other people. He's the guy who is extremely humble. And an extremely bright human being and a caring man. And, so I look at those qualities and I try to emulate them. And I try to bring those things into my process and apply them to AA when sponsoring people, and to business, and to mentoring.

So there's a defining way of how I line people up and judge them. And how I judge what their actions and their words really mean. Some people are going to sit there and tell you what they're going to do but they don't do it. What's that say? When a guy cancels his appointment with you and doesn't call. And now we're a day after the scheduled time before he reaches out. They don't really value that relationship with you.

I know when I'm going to meet with my mentor that I'm counting the days down. I can't wait to meet with him. I look forward to when I see him next because I know my business acumen is going to be raised every time I see him. And I'm going to become a better leader; I'm going to become a better human being. I'm going to become a better person for my community and my family. And that's what I think what happens in a successful relationship like that. I care about the guy. The guy's an incredible, incredible guy.

But when I've been asked to do the same with some entrepreneurs, they're not interested. They're just not. What

entrepreneurs

they want to do is they want to be patted on the back for things they're doing well. They don't want to have any sort of objections to anything they're doing. I'm not their father. Right, I'm not here to scold them. I'm not here to tell them they probably shouldn't do that long-term, they should probably think about it, what they're doing right there. I think that's when you get back to emotional intelligence, being self-aware of who you are.

So you have to ask yourself do you really want a mentor. Or do you really just want to tell people you have a mentor? Because if you ask people and do this, and ask people if they have a mentor they'll say they do. And you'll ask how many times do you meet with them? And If they're meeting with their mentor six times a year they have a mentor. If they're like I haven't met with my mentor in two years they don't have a mentor. Because those same people who cancel meetings, at least from my perspective I understood that I'm not important in their life.

They're the same people who cancel and say hey, can we do it next week instead? My response to that is to tell them you find a date. I'm not doing that. You find a date. You let me know and I'll let you know if it works or not and then get back to you. And I ask myself was the relationship that important?

Everything you've heard me say today, in the past say, how long have we talked, five minutes about this? You understand that my relationship with my mentor is extremely important. You know, he doesn't even know he was one of the catalysts for me going and getting an MBA. He said something to me like go get your MBA because as long as I've known you nothing's ever gotten in your way.

entrepreneurs

And we ended it right there. And then we didn't meet for like four months. And during those four months I applied and got into the EMBA program at Fox Temple. And so then we met in like November or something. And I said guess what in January I'm starting at Temple's Fox School of business and I'm going to get my MBA, the executive program.

And he went, "what?"
I said, "yeah, guess what?"
He says, "what are you talking about?"
I said, "you told me to do it."
He goes, "I did?"
I said, "well you didn't necessarily say go do it but if you said, if I was worried about running my business when it was $15 million dollars or whatever, you said go get your MBA, so I did."
He goes, "and they accepted you?"
And I'm like, "yeah."
And he reacted like it was the greatest story he's ever heard. He just told me it was incredible and that he couldn't believe just like that I went and did it. Based on an offhand comment he didn't remember. I said well I asked. And then I followed through and they saw benefit of having me there you know or they wouldn't have me there. And he told that he felt like the benefit I was going to bring was immense.

And these are his words not mine, "they're getting an entrepreneur who's doing everything that they're talking about. Why wouldn't they want to have you in the class?"

Carlos: I would agree with that statement. He's absolutely right. I mean that's why I'm talking to you. I don't know

entrepreneurs

what I'm doing. I don't know how to run a business. I've never done it before. But I do know that I'm asking the smartest people know the right questions. I believe that everyone else has way more experience in this world than I do and that experience can benefit me. And then even better I can use that to benefit someone else.

Sean McDermott: *I don't feel like I know any more than anyone else. I think my experience is what carries me at this point.*

take away

If you ever meet Sean, he's a very likeable person. I implied it in the introduction but he has the physical presence of a linebacker, but he is one of the most polite, soft spoken, and kind individuals I've meet. I'm not certain if his personality drives his humility or his humility drives his personality but either way you can't help but want to know more about him. What I also love about Sean, that is ever present during the interview is his resiliency. He shared a very personal aspect of his life in confronting his addiction. He was able to overcome those stumbles in his life and still achieve a high degree of personal and professional success. It's something I've seen from many entrepreneurs and leaders in general: the ability to make mistakes, take responsibility for them, and accept the consequences for those mistakes. But it goes beyond that. A good leader, a good business owner will then learn from those experiences and grow beyond them.

I believe this is important aspect to being a human but I have found this ability to be highly developed in

entrepreneurs

effective leaders, and successful entrepreneurs. An extreme example of this is Steve Jobs. Love him or hate him, Jobs lead Apple into a billion dollar company by the age of 30 only to be unceremoniously fired. In a speech he gave at a commencement in 2005 at Stanford University he is quoted as saying, *"What had been the focus of my entire adult life was gone, and it was devastating. [...] I was a very public failure."* He was resilient. He learned. He went on to found NeXT (which was subsequently purchased by Apple) and purchase Pixar (from George Lucas) and as history tells us 11 years later he returned to Apple and was appointed CEO. Again.

There's also a humility to admitting your failings. This humbleness parallels what we discussed earlier as a trait identified in Cathy. She had the humble self awareness to recognize she would need to ask for help some some of the more technical aspects of her non-profit. Humility seems to be a common trait among successful leaders, and successful business owners. Sean also demonstrates this trait in spades. He owns and accepts his past and uses it everyday to guide his decisions. Rather than constantly viewing his past struggles as a negative, he leverages his experience to connect with others, to have empathy and understanding, to lead. In short he accepted responsibility for his mistakes. He also learned from them, and he uses that knowledge as fuel to drive his success.

A year out from the interview I thought about what I had learned from Sean is how humble he is and how he uses that to drive passion for success. His willingness to do any manner of job he was qualified to do, and to learn

entrepreneurs

how to do jobs he wasn't yet qualified to do. My favorite quote from our discussion is, *"you wanted to pay me to sweep your floor, I would've swept your floor, it didn't matter."* He is the CEO of his company but he doesn't view himself as being above anything in order to achieve success in his own eyes. For me this quote represents his drive to succeed encapsulated in words.

It's his brand of work ethic, humble confidence, and resiliency that enables Sean to attract quality talent to his firm and drive engagement. Through his strong leadership he was able to successfully grow his business. This is a practical demonstration of the real business value Sean's style of leadership enables. He said it best, *"wealth is a symptom of doing a good job."* Well Sean is doing a good job at being both a leader, and an entrepreneur.

entrepreneurs

Joe Chavarria: New Generation Graphics

I didn't want to interview my dad because I was seeking catharsis for some unresolved issue. I wanted to interview my dad because he's an extremely savvy businessman and he's my hero. I didn't have a full appreciation for that growing up. I wasn't a bad kid generally. I didn't have behavioral problems in school. I got good grades for the most part, which was primarily because my parents emphasized the importance of education. But I wasn't exactly a good person. I was selfish. I was lazy. I didn't appreciate everything my parents did for me which lasted into my mid 20's. So maybe in that sense I was an average, immature, angst filled kid. But after enlisting in the military I finally understood why family was so important. That's when I really started to appreciate everything my parents had done for me. That's when I realized how lucky I was to have such strong role models in my life. For all the emphasis people put on privileges these days I have the biggest advantage in life that anyone can have: two parents who love me. And because of that love they taught me the value of education, they taught me to work hard (even if I didn't always heed that lesson), and they taught me to care about people around me (even though I didn't always heed that lesson either).

I come from a family of immigrants. My paternal great grandfather was born in the city of La Cruz, in Chihuahua, Mexico around 1865. He immigrated to the United States via El Paso, Texas. His signature is in the border crossing logbook: 10 March 1914, Longino

entrepreneurs

Chavarria, 5 children. My grandfather, Longino Chavarria Jr. was born in Las Cruces, New Mexico on 14 August 1914. My father was born in Bakersfield, California in September 1949. He grew up speaking Spanish, and learned English in school. This was 1950's and 1960's California. This was during the height of Cesar Chavez and the formation of what would become the United Farm Workers. The Delano grape strike was in 1965 and Bakersfield is a short 30 miles to the South. As a result of Chavez's activism, Spanish speakers and specifically Mexicans were viewed as troublemakers. People with brown skin were agitators and outsiders seeking to upset the status quo. It was a much different time in California.

My father is very gifted at math. He earned his degree in accounting and worked as a CPA for a time. He always did very well in math but in California in the 1960's if you were brown and you spoke Spanish you were given shop class and told to move along. There was no expectation for achievement. There were no programs to encourage or develop the talents your teachers might have recognized.

None of these things are meant to be an indictment on society or the education system during that time period by any means. This is just scenery building. So you can understand the circumstances my father was handed. But those circumstances are part and parcel to why my dad is such an exceptional human, and why I appreciate him so much.

So despite my dad's natural affinity for mathematics he was steered away from college. It was the Vietnam era. My dad wasn't college bound. And on 20 November 1968

entrepreneurs

my father was drafted into the U.S. Army. He would become an airborne infantryman. After basic training and jump school, he was assigned to the 82nd Airborne. If you are ever afforded the opportunity to meet my father and get a chance to really get to know him, he is filled with great stories from this time in his life. Ask him about how sound travels when floating in a parachute.

After his time in the military my dad went through a rough period in a battle with addiction. More than just social drinking, his life became entangled with drug use and addiction. For those of you reading this and have experienced life in or around addiction you know what a destructive force it can be. When my mom got pregnant with my sister he stopped. He decided to kick his drug habit the day he found out my mom was pregnant. He decided that his future wife and daughter were more important than his addiction.

He still drank and for several more years it became alcohol that filled up his addictive behaviors, and then in 1983 when I was about 3 years old he decided to quit drinking as well. I have very strong and distinct memories of going to NA and AA meetings as a child. I remember sneaking coffee and donuts from the folding tables they brought out at the churches we would go to. I remember playing soccer in the grass lots outside Calvary Bible Church with the other kids. I remember Isabel, and Micah, and Jordan, and some of the other friends I made. I didn't understand why we went to these meetings until much later. I didn't appreciate their value until even later than that. I remember when my dad got his 5 year chip. And then his 10 year chip. And then his 20 year chip. My

entrepreneurs

dad has been clean and sober for more than 30 years and I am so proud of him.

Despite working more than full time to help support our family he attended night school so he could finish his bachelor's degree. Despite battling addiction he worked, and saved, and bought a house. Despite all the challenges he had faced both internal and external, despite everything he had already accomplished, in 2004 my dad started his own company after 18 years in the screen printing industry and as you'll read he's been very successful. Just getting by was never okay. My dad knows the value of hard work and he understands the importance of education. With my mom's help he even managed to raise a couple of pretty okay kids. My sister might argue she turned out better and she's probably right. This was the last interview I did and I hope you think my dad is cooler than your dad. Because he is. Enjoy!

entrepreneurs

ɸ

Carlos: This will be a little bit weird because you're my dad. I already know a lot of the answers for the questions I usually ask but let's start with the basics. What is your business and when did you start your business?

Joe Chavarria: *New Generation Graphics. It's a t-shirt printing company and we got started in 2004.*

Carlos: And how'd you get into printing t-shirts?

Joe Chavarria: *When I went back to school to finish college I needed a part-time job. Somebody gave me a part-time job printing t-shirts.*

Carlos: Did you think then that you'd be still be doing it in thirty years?

Joe Chavarria: *No. Not at all. I actually went to school to be an accountant and that's what I earned my degree in, but I found that I really liked the screen printing industry so I decided to stick with it.*

Carlos: Do you think your accounting degree helped you with running your business now?

Joe Chavarria: *Yeah. Absolutely. My education taught me, or it gave me an understanding of money and working capital. About not spending more than what you're making as a business. Which is important.*

Carlos: I remember growing up you worked as an accountant for a little bit. You worked for an accounting firm? That would have been around the late 80's.

Joe Chavarria: *Yeah, it would have been '88, '89 maybe. For about six months I worked for an accounting firm.*

Carlos: Wasn't for you? Going a partner track and working a typical 9 to 5?

entrepreneurs

Joe Chavarria: *No, not really. Corporate culture was a little bit different back then. The structure was a little bit; I was older and the structure that they had was built for younger kids coming out of college. It was an extremely competitive environment. They, well they kind of pitted you against each other.*

Carlos: They didn't really emphasize teamwork. Not as much as today anyway.

Joe Chavarria: *No, there was no teamwork. It was very individualistic. If you were able to step on the guy that was a little bit ahead of you and jump over him, well they kind of encouraged that and it was expected. It was very cut throat, very much dog-eat-dog.*

Carlos: Yeah. That's weird to hear with today's lens. Now things are somewhat different at least on the surface. They're trying to make strides to get people to work together more. I think some of the newer tech companies like Google and Facebook, and all tech companies really are driving away from that. I think you started to see that when millennials entered into the workforce. They're a little bit different than the folks coming out of business school in the '80's I think.

But is that toxic culture what pushed you to open your own business? You said you had been working in the industry for a while. What drove the decision to become small business owner?

Joe Chavarria: *Well I worked for a company for 18 years starting as the part-time guy and working my way up to operations and general manager and I was let go from there. I was already 55 by then, and I moped around the house for a day or so and finally your mom told me I need*

entrepreneurs

to go find a job. So I went out the next day and I got a job in another company but it was in outside sales. I already knew a lot of people in the industry. And I already knew other customers that I always helped previously doing inside sales so I started going out on cold calls. It was a lot of cold calls. I would call up the people I knew and ask if I could go see them and they would say well come on out. After a while of doing that slowly but surely I developed relationships with them and they kept giving me business.

So I was working at this company for almost a year. But I realized that the people they had in their production couldn't or wouldn't produce the quality I needed to keep customers happy. The person they had running their production didn't like change. There were some things they were doing that were no longer industry best practice and just because it was good enough 20 years ago doesn't mean that it's good enough today. The industry had changed. The technology had changed, and I needed them to kind of move forward. There were better ways to print and they weren't willing to hear that or grow with the industry.

It came to a point where it was a constant struggle to ensure quality and I just didn't want to be fighting with somebody who didn't understand that there were better ways to do things. And so I came home one day and looked at your mom and we talked. I said I can stay here and I don't mind getting paid what I'm getting paid. I said it's going to be a dog fight every day, and I think I can do this better. And she said well we've been poor before.

So we stepped out and I started researching equipment that I already knew well but I started

entrepreneurs

researching the manufacturers of the equipment to see where I was going to be able to spend the least amount and the get the maximum amount of value from what I had. I partnered up with a person and we were able to open the business. The unfortunate part about it is that my partner, they didn't help me through any of the process. They just thought the money was just going to pour in and they didn't have to do anything. That is very rarely the case or everyone would do it.

So after a couple of years they asked me to buy them out and I did. I gave them their money back and that was probably, at least in terms of timing that was the best thing that ever happened. Because after that the company just exploded and we were doing numbers that I probably wouldn't have been able to buy them out after that. So it happened at the right time and I haven't looked back. We've been through a couple of tough years but I haven't really looked back in terms of wanting to just hang it up or quit the business or stop doing what I'm doing.

Carlos: What do you think the biggest difference in going from inside sales to outside sales was?

Joe Chavarria: *There's more of a risk because I was making cold calls. I had to call people I didn't know. I would call people that I knew and I'd ask them who were the decision makers at certain places or I'd ask somebody who was doing the buying for a certain company. Or who I needed to talk to at a certain company and they would tell me and I would go over there and ask to see them in person. Sometimes it worked. Sometimes I'd have to make another appointment and go back and see them. But I had to get over the idea that just because I didn't know them or*

entrepreneurs

it was a cold call that they weren't going to want to talk to me. So I just had to do it.

Carlos: Was there ever a time that you wanted to just quit on the business? Just end the day thinking all right, I'm out, I've got to get out of this.

Joe Chavarria: *Never. There were times when it was real difficult, and I think a couple of years in 2009 to 2010 where I wasn't sure we'd survive. Those two years were just extremely stressful. For everybody I think. Just because everybody was in the same boat, businesses, schools, governments. There was no busy time at the shop. There was no business. It was hard to get any kind of money to continue to business. So we just kind of eked it out and managed to get through to the other side of those two years. Those two years were just brutal for everybody. After that though things became easier because we were ready to go and we knew we could survive. Once business started picking back up and we weren't one of the companies that had to restart everything things started rolling. We were already geared up. We benefited from that.*

Carlos: Do you think your ability to manage money was the difference maker in that, during those times?

Joe Chavarria: *I think so. I think that we survived because we were managing our money well. The other thing we did is that we were talking to our vendors and letting them know where we were at. Constant communication. So they were able to extend terms on what we were buying and we were able to make it past those two years*

Carlos: So that's a big one. You said you worked with your vendors. You talked with them and communicated with them. Do you think building those personal relationships

entrepreneurs

with the people that you're getting your products from is an important part of your business?

Joe Chavarria: *I think the more you can foster that relationship the better. The better relationship you have with your vendors then if you ever run into a situation where you are going to need them to kind of support you a little bit they will be more likely willing to do it than not. Because you're selling their products so both of you can make money. So if you don't have any contact with them; if you're not constantly talking with them either through your rep that you deal with you're hurting business. If you're not on good terms with them; if they don't see you at the trade shows then they don't know you. They haven't built that partnership with you. But if you take the time to do those things then they're more willing to try to help you out when you get into a tough situation. I think that's one of the things that helped us survive.*

Carlos: You talked about going to a trade show a little bit. You just got back from that last weekend; you were down in Long Beach. How long have you been going down there and how important is that event to your business?

Joe Chavarria: *I've been going to that trade show for 28 years now and it's extremely important. I know a lot of companies and businesses in our industry don't view it as being important but I like to take my employees down there for the day to let them see what the industry is. That's important because it's a global, multi-billion dollar industry. And once they see that, and they start understanding what the potential for the work and the career in this industry is; they tend to want to apply themselves.*

entrepreneurs

For us it's also to make contact with the people that we're doing business with. We're also looking at new ideas, new procedures whether it be a new marketing strategies or channels, or a new product that's come out that's going to make our business a little bit stronger; that's why I go down there; because nobody comes up here. We're in Bakersfield. We're not a big market like LA or San Francisco. It's hard to get a sales guy to come and visit us. So most of the time when we can go down there and capture them in a trade show where you have everybody in one spot, and we can spend a day or two just talking with everyone and looking at new products, new equipment; I think that's very important.

Carlos: Speaking of new equipment when you went down there this year you actually just made a capital investment back into your business. How do you make those decisions on when it's time?

Joe Chavarria: *Well I look at our equipment age and how much it's costing us to maintain. Our current press has lasted all fourteen years I've been in business but it's like anything else it starts wearing down. Recently we started having more issues with it. It started breaking down a little bit more often which slows down production. The parts started becoming an issue because they're harder to source.*

If you think about it the machine hasn't been in production for several years. So when I make a decision that I need to upgrade our equipment or make a capital investment those are the things that I look at. Total cost of ownership. It's not just the purchase price; it's also equipment maintenance, and it's reliability. If the machine

entrepreneurs

breaks down I have to pay to get it repaired but I also am still paying my employees for that day but they're not finishing orders so that drives up our production costs. So I think about all of those things and that's how I determine whether it's time to get new equipment.

Carlos: What do you think the biggest challenge for you so far has been in terms of running the business?

Joe Chavarria: *The biggest challenge is employees. It's hard to find employees. Hiring someone is getting more and more difficult. Most employees, most people that apply for the positions we have are wanting huge sums of money right away. These are entry level roles generally so we're training them to do the job we need them to do while we pay them. Every position we have you can work yourself up to a certain salary. But from what I've experienced the younger applicants have the mentality that somehow we're a startup computer company, or an app company, or someplace where they make mega bucks and that's not necessarily the case. They want $30 bucks an hour to fold t-shirts and that's just not going to happen. It's not realistic and not even affordable for us as a business. So we run into that quite often.*

    Then we run into people that don't have any work skills. They don't know how to show up on time or worse refuse to show up on time. They don't understand that they actually have to come in and do work.

Carlos: I know you say, or you're very upfront with your employees and let them know they're not going to be a millionaire working at one of the entry level jobs. The roles you normally need aren't highly skilled tradecraft roles, and they don't require advanced professional degrees or

entrepreneurs

years of specialized education. As a result your leadership and HR strategy can be different than say a hospital might view staffing or how a manufacturing plant might need machinists or electricians. How do you view leading employees that you have because much of your workforce is in an entry level role?

Joe Chavarria: *For me it's trying to help them understand that regardless of what they have planned for the future that they have to work and learn as much about what they're doing now; because they don't want wake up one day and its five years later and they haven't applied themselves and they're still at entry-level pay. It's what I tell all the employees. I tell them all the time that no matter where you're at or what you're doing you should try to do your best because you never know what comes next in your life.*

I try to tell them or more accurately I try to educate them as much as possible, and I try to help them understand why certain things are important. I try and share my life experiences and the things I've learned from my mistakes. One of the biggest things I do is I give them pointers of how you can make more money as an employee because that's important to them. I'm very upfront with them and explain to them that there are only a handful of jobs in the company that will that allow you to support a family and those roles are currently filled with people who probably aren't planning on leaving.

I also ask them questions just have an understanding about where they want to go and what they want to do. So I'll ask them if they want to stay in the industry that we're in. If they say yes and they want to make a living and have

entrepreneurs

a family I let them know what they need to do. Now they have a direction and now they're going to have to learn as much about our industry as they possibly can. And when it comes time they can open up their own business and have one of the jobs where they can support a family. But if they don't learn anything about what they're doing now, then when it comes time for them to decide what they want to do next, then opening their own business in the screen printing industry or embroidery is not going to be realistic. It's not going to be an option because they're not going to know enough because they didn't invest the time now.

Carlos: You've mentioned being employees needing to be "on time" a number of times. Do you think that comes from your time in the Army? Because I don't think I valued or at least understood the importance of being on time until after I joined the military.

Joe Chavarria: *I think that's part of it. I think that the discipline that you have to have as a business owner that should trickle down to your employees and it should be leadership by example. So if I was always late they'd learn that behavior was acceptable. Or if I was never in the back reminding them or helping them understand why being on time is important, if I just let it go and didn't say anything then I think we'd be in a mess. The business would be much worse off.*

Because when they're late it slows down the team. It's disrespectful to their teammates who showed up on time. Even though they can make up the time by staying late, maybe one of their coworkers can't and they need the team to run the jobs. You know maybe they have to pick up their kid or they have a parent teacher conference or a

entrepreneurs

medical appointment and can't stay late. It becomes an imposition. These are things I don't think people consider or keep in the front of their mind when they think it's not really a big deal. And maybe it isn't one or two times but overall, it hurts their team, it hurts morale, and it hurts the business. So I like being on time and I like people to be on time.

Carlos: So you brought discipline, being on time, being respectful, you brought those characteristics into the business world with you. How do you translate those military skills from the rigid hierarchical structure military life engenders, to the private business world where people can walk away? That's one of the differences between a regular job and joining the military. The government won't let you quit. You can't just walk away from them. So barking orders or transactional leadership loses its effectiveness over time. Not to say that's always the leadership strategy for military leaders but it is certainly far more prevalent.

Joe Chavarria: *Well I think if you're consistent with your message about the types of positive behaviors you want from the very beginning you'll have success in fostering that type of culture. For example from the very beginning we have an employee handbook that deals with all of the issues that can come up in terms of being on time, your time off, and what you can expect from us as a business. The things that we promise you are all in there whether it be vacation or, or your holidays that you're going to take off. And then of course all the things that the State of California, the government requires us to do. In fact in just in the last*

entrepreneurs

couple of years we've had to give all employees three paid sick days a year.

Which I don't mind doing that. I don't have a problem with that at all. I think it's a good thing to do. But somewhere along the line we have to be able to make that productivity back up. When you're talking 15 employees and they all get three days of sick pay. That's about five or six thousand dollars in pay, plus wage taxes and all the associated costs that go into total costs for employing someone that I didn't have to give out three or four years ago. So I tell the employees that somewhere along the line we have to get that back. Maybe we have to increase our prices. And it's not always just necessarily raising the price of a shirt or our price of the goods that we're selling. It could be gains in how efficient we are. Maybe we can make it up by making fewer mistakes; cutting down on our mistakes.

Those kinds of things are cumulative. Small gains that add up and when you combine them all together they kind of offset that increased cost. So the employees can have their three days, and I'm glad to give it to them. I'm glad we can all work better and work together to provide that as an employer because I mean some of them have kids and the kids get sick so they have to take time off and I just think it makes it easier for them. Anything I can do to make their job easier, their lives easier is what I'm trying to do.

Carlos: And you do a lot for your employees outside of pay. I remember four years ago you took all your employees up to San Francisco for the weekend. Not just your employees but some family friends as well, and I flew out too. But you took them to a baseball game and you

entrepreneurs

put them up in the hotel for the weekend, paid for transportation. It was to celebrate your first 10 years in business and you wanted to reward your team; some of who had been with you for all 10 years. How do you come up with those kinds of ideas? What other things do you do to kind of drive employee morale and kind of give back to your team?

Joe Chavarria: *Well we try to get better at what we're doing for them in terms of how we communicate and show recognition and appreciation. This year instead of having our regular Christmas party at the office we actually rented a venue and did a really nice job in presenting them a place that was special for the company Christmas party. We really wanted to treat them, and show them we appreciate the work they do all year, and they were all blown away because it was such a better setting.*

Carlos: I see the pictures that Corrine puts up and it's not just Christmas parties. All year you might throw a big barbecue for them on a weekend or you might buy them lunch randomly. And when I talk to you and Corrine I know you had a party for someone's new baby or to celebrate a birthday. You do a family day event and you always do Fourth of July. And there's food and it's personal. You are literally cooking the food for your employees. You put a lot of personal effort into these events, and not just into these events but into your company. Do you think the employees appreciate those little things? Do you think it adds value in terms of team building? And outside of employee morale do you think you get a tangible return on investment as well?

entrepreneurs

Joe Chavarria: *Yeah. Absolutely. Most of the employees appreciate that stuff. I think that everybody tries a little bit harder. Because they know we're trying to provide a little bit more for them, so they try a little bit harder and I see that. If all of my employees make one less mistake or take just that little bit extra to make sure a job is right, it'll save the company money, time, reputation. That's the business return part of it but there's more to it than that.*

I've always thought that you have to be able to do that stuff regardless of where you're at. I mean, as a small company we try to do as much and I mean as much as we possibly can for employees because they don't call it work for nothing. I mean they have to come to work but at the same time, and I tell them all the time it doesn't always have to just be come to work, punch a clock and then be sad faced all day. You can enjoy your job. No matter else what's going on in your life when you come to work it should be your sanctuary.

It shouldn't be a place of dread or anxiety. You come to work and there's nobody hassling you. There's nobody breathing down your neck. Your problems are still going to be there when you get off work, but at least you're not carrying them. You have the ability to leave your outside world at the door and then just try to enjoy the day there. You spend eight hours a day working there. It should be a place where you want to go not a place you dread going.

And because most of the stuff we're doing the people like the job. We don't micromanage them. Everybody has the ability to make decisions about how they approach their job. They can speak up and are encouraged to do so. I just think it makes for a more involved employee. A more

entrepreneurs

engaged employee that's going to be a little bit more attentive to the work that they're doing. If an issue comes up they're just not going to go along with it. They're going to speak up about it. They're going to raise their hand. They're going to say, "This doesn't look right."

Of course we didn't start there. It's been a long struggle to get there and for me to understand why it's important. In the past I think before we got to this point I think they just kind of just went along. It didn't matter whether it looked right or not. They just went ahead and did what they were told and didn't question anything.

Carlos: When did you realize that was important? Or how did you kind of foster that sort of environment? I don't imagine it just grew overnight or that you knew that it was the right thing to do from day one.

Joe Chavarria: *Well you have to start taking a look at yourself as people manager. On how you're managing the people what you're doing wrong as a leader. You have to be a leader not just a manager, and not just the boss, or the owner. It took me a long time understand that about employees, about people.*

It's more than just telling them what to do. It's being able to understanding them, and their lives, and that they matter too. If someone is having an issue with one of their kids or their family it's going to affect them. It's that you understand their needs and that they're a person. It's that you know their kids' names, and that you take interest in their lives. You know that they're not just robots that just show up to work and they're working for you and you don't care what goes on in their lives. If they're having a hard time, if one of their kids is sick, then we try to help them

entrepreneurs

along. We either give them extra time off or just pay them for the day if they need to leave early or come in late, or whatever issue is going on in their lives.

For example we have an employee now who has several family members that experienced a tragic accident and will be hospitalized for months. And so they haven't been coming to work because they needed time off. They could have used FMLA and taken unpaid leave but they have bills and can't afford to go unpaid for the whole time. So we presented an idea to the staff and they were able to give up one of their sick days to help them. We just talked to the employees and said if anybody was willing to do that and most of them gave up a day. Most of them were able to give up one of their sick days which is all we allowed. Just in case they get sick.

And this was an extraordinary circumstance it wasn't just a bad flu or something. This was pretty bad. And everybody on the team knows that. But we made it clear to everyone, I said once they goes through that donated time, then as a company we'll step up and do a couple of things for them above and beyond that. A lot of them signed up and they signed a sick day over to the affected employee and they have been able to get a full check for the last four weeks. And then once that runs out then we'll step in and help them as a company. The company will do its part and work with them to see what they need and get those needs addressed. Because they still need to get a paycheck to support their family and pay their bills. At the same time they have to be at the hospital with their impacted family members as much as possible.

entrepreneurs

So we worked as a community, we worked together as a team, because we're all in this together. And hopefully in a few more weeks things will be straightened out a little bit and they can return to work. But it's going to be a grueling process for everyone involved, mentally and physically so we want to support them and their family as much as possible. So you have to take all of that stuff into consideration and just try to do the best you can. And when people see you doing those things then they really know, and they believe you care about them. And we do, and that's the bottom line that counts. We as a company, and really everybody talks about family and teamwork and how important they are. But at the end of the day if you're not actually practicing that stuff what good is it?

Carlos: What do you think your biggest success so far has been in terms of running the company?

Joe Chavarria: *Being able to keep the company in business for fourteen years. We started it ... When I started the company we didn't really have working capital to speak of. We just kind of had to make it work with what we had until we gradually built up to where we're at now. We don't struggle as much as we used to. But we still have to be careful about how we spend our money.*

Carlos: And do you have a busy season or an off season?

Joe Chavarria: *The busiest time of the year for us is from August into mid-December. We probably do almost two thirds of our annual business during that time period.*

Carlos: Have you looked at ways to develop some of that business earlier in the year to try and even out your throughput? Or just drive more sales outside of that quarter?

entrepreneurs

Joe Chavarria: *Well we're constantly looking at that. I mean we're always looking to upgrade our customer base. One of our problems has been is that the economy is up and down. The economy here is centered on the energy sector. There's a lot of oil field work here. The petroleum industry is a large portion of our local economy. So when they're down then we don't get that work because it's all a big cycle; it's an ecosystem. And it seems like a lot of the bigger companies are moving out of California. I see that in how our customers have changed over the years.*

So we kind of have to adjust who we're trying to sell our products to. And we are constantly upgrading our product selection. We're expanding from just printing t-shirts, and embroidering shirts and hats, but also offering promotional products like pins and mugs. Those kinds of things help us along with our sales by providing another revenue channel we can capture customers with.

Carlos: What's your least favorite thing about owning a business?

Joe Chavarria: *The least favorite thing about having my own business is managing employees. Having to deal with all the personalities is a lot of work. Each employee has their own personality and I can't approach them the same way. There's not a cookie cutter program, or whatever you want to call it that applies to each and every one of them. There's no single way to treat them or one leadership style that you can just blanket them all with.*

So you have to engage with every one of them a little bit different and you have to be able to understand that. It's very tough to figure that out for each employee. There's a learning curve and you're going to make a lot of mistakes

entrepreneurs

and it can be a big ego check. But again if invest the time now and do it the right way then it becomes easier to lead them and that's the pay off.

Carlos: Other side of that, what has been your favorite thing about owning your own business so far?

Joe Chavarria: *Being able to help people. Not just our employees but also different charities in the community.*

Carlos: Do you want to talk about that a little bit? I think it's fair to get a little recognition for your employees I'm sure they'd appreciate it.

Joe Chavarria: *Well I never look to profit from people's misery. So sometimes people ask us for different things because one of their family members has passed away or something and we'll try to help them as much as possible. We don't ask anything back from them. Sometimes that means we'll print an order for them for just the cost of goods.*

We work with the local fire departments on some of their programs and they ask us to donate certain items and we're almost always able to provide that support for them. We do a lot of work with the schools in the Bakersfield area and really all of Kern County. A lot of times their programs don't have any money or are severely underfunded and they'll ask us to help them along. We always try and help them as much as possible as well. Schools and education are important. So in those cases we'll donate the shirts or provide them at a significantly lower price, or find another solution so we can help out.

And I think all of those things in the end they foster goodwill. People appreciate that and I think that's the key for us. That's a core part of our business operations and

entrepreneurs

reputation. It's what drives the loyalty that we get from a lot of customers, and I feel like that has been one of the biggest reasons why we have been successful. It's why so many people like us because we will always try to help. And we're just a small company. We're just a small company. We all live in this community. We try to help each other. Obviously I still have to make a profit to stay in business so I can provide jobs for people to earn a living and I understand that part of it but I'm not trying to squeeze people for every little dime.

When somebody comes up and they need some help then we'll talk it over and decide what we want to do. I don't make the decisions by myself anymore. I have Corrine, and Kip, and Sam, and Monica. Sometimes we'll get together and talk about what would be the best way to help somebody. It's not always about donating money. Sometimes we can set up a program for people so students can order shirts and we carry the inventory costs. That can be a difference maker in schools that don't have funding for some of the after school programs. So we try and look at things a lot of different ways to find the right solution.

Carlos: So you just mentioned four names. Are they your leadership team for the company? How long have they been working for you?

Joe Chavarria: *Yes. Sam has been working for me since the beginning. Kip, has been working for us for about seven or eight years. Monica, about five or six, and obviously Corrine (Corrine is my sister) started with me when I opened the business so she's also been there from the very beginning.*

entrepreneurs

Carlos: And you're getting ready to take a lesser role. How do you feel about that?

Joe Chavarria: *Well I have confidence that they're going to be able to get things done. I have actually have taken my hands off a lot of stuff. I let them take charge over a lot of the day to day stuff and more of the decision making. I have let them take their bumps and bruises on some of the things that have come up, because again I'm not micromanaging them. They have more control and make more decisions. Part of that means they might stumble over some things but I think it's a valuable learning tool. And this has been coming for the last three, four years. It was this last year I just kind of like let them trip up more and allow them to problem solve. And if I see that it's going to damage the company or damage our reputation a bit then I'll step in and get things back on track.*

Carlos: Do you think that's an important part of the learning process for them to develop as leaders?

Joe Chavarria: *Yes, I do. You can't always just keep doing stuff for people. It's what I tell them, you have to speak up. You have to. In order to get to the next level or the next stage of your life in terms of how you earn more money is being a leader. You have to be the person that directs. Even if you don't have the title if you're doing that work at some point in time you're going to have to be paid for that.*

So if you're constantly helping the people around you do their jobs properly or pushing them to learn more or get better then we see that. I see that. And when someone does that then I believe we need to give that person a raise because I see them doing all this stuff. Now that's extra

entrepreneurs

stuff aside from what they're doing for themselves. So to me that's important. And I recognize those things.

You know some of the employees are kind of young and they're afraid to speak up but I tell them you can't let that fear of speaking out or sounding stupid, you can't let that keep you from trying to improve yourself.

Carlos: What do you think is one of the more important things that you try and help your employees understand? And how do you communicate that message down to them? Because people forget, we all forget things. I think we all get into a routine over time as we get more comfortable and confident in our jobs, and we need little reminders about why certain things are important.

Joe Chavarria: *I think the biggest thing that I tell them is that there is nobody out there who is just giving away things for free. There's no such thing as a free lunch. Nobody gives me anything and I don't expect anybody to give me free product or come in and do work on my equipment for free. If a technician comes in to make a repair I don't expect him to come in and do it for free. I don't ask my employees to come and work for free. My expectation is that they come in and work and then I need to pay them. At the same time because I employ them and I do pay them there are expectations from them as well. I expect them to show up on time, that's part of why I pay them. I expect them to do their work and I expect them to do their work at a high level, that's part of why I pay them. So for me the deal is that things are not a one way street.*

How I communicate that is I have a staff meeting every Monday morning and in that staff meeting depending on what is scheduled to come up that week we talk about

entrepreneurs

different topics. A lot of the things that I talk about are how you become better as an employee; how you can make more money; what my expectations are from everybody there in terms of how you come to work. I expect people to be on time. It might sound minor to some people but if you're one minute late you're late. I don't make that excuse for myself and I'm not going to make it for them.

So I'm not looking over their shoulder. Again I'm not micromanaging them. I'm not their babysitter. But I know who comes and goes at certain times. You know that's one thing that I've always kind of been aware of. I communicate from day one being on time is one of the things that to me is very important. And they know that's the expectation and we're constantly talking about the behaviors that are important.

We're also constantly talking about what our goals are as a company and what our mission statement is so the team understands what we should be focusing on doing: delivering quality product for our customer on time.

Carlos: Your mission statement is very customer centric. That's Amazon's focus. Their mission statement is something like, to be the most customer centric company in the world. Apple is the same way. A lot of very successful companies have this mentality and approach. But you don't have to be customer centric to be successful. There are companies and industries that don't take that approach.

How did you come to pick that strategy? Because I was at Starbucks yesterday and I ran into one of your customers. They saw I was wearing a New Generation sweatshirt and they approached me while I was waiting for

entrepreneurs

my coffee. They came up to me and said, "*I absolutely love New Generation Graphics. I think it's the best company there is in the city.*" They were very excited about the company but also you as a person. They said that you were just an amazing person. How have you fostered that sort of reputation? It seems that your customers are extremely loyal, extremely responsive to what you've done. You can't buy that type of reaction, you have to build that. How did you get there? How did you build that type of reputation?

Joe Chavarria: *It's a direct result of implementing our mission statement. I always thought and I believe it is important to deliver the products on time. So if you say you're going to have it to them on Tuesday in a week then you better have it on Tuesday in a week. Keeping your word with the customer consistently means you're reliable. That's something I think everyone appreciates.*

Being able to be a little flexible with our customers is also important them. Anybody can say no. I mean to the customer, anybody can say no. Especially when it was a customer mistake it's easy for a company to say no. But I think that one of the things that makes us stick out; makes a difference in how people view us. If I can get a customer request done when somebody comes in and says hey I need this shirt, I forgot it my order or I need some shirts in a couple of days. If there is a way for me to get it done I am going to get it done. More often than not we are able to get people out of emergencies.

Anybody can do the work if given a couple of weeks. The standard two week turn around for an order. I don't care what company it is. Most of the companies in town

entrepreneurs

that are in the industry if you give them two weeks they can get it out. It's the other stuff. The little things like when somebody forgets or when they have an emergency and they come and ask you if you can bail them out. If you're able to be responsive and provide that service it goes a long way. I try and do that all the time and keep that mentality. And that fosters loyalty.

Carlos: How do you grow your business? How do you drive sales? Is it all word of mouth? I'm sure that reputation of reliability and approachability helps.

Joe Chavarria: *It does help because it's all word of mouth. Well a lot of word of mouth. That's one of the areas we're behind a little bit on. For instance we should have a functional website. We have a website but we're not managing it properly. We're not advertising on it. We're not giving specials on it. So in that respect we're behind the curve. So all the new channels that you can use to market your business whether it's through Facebook, Twitter, Instagram, Google, we're behind in that. And I realize that and it's one of the areas I've been trying to work on. But we just haven't gotten to the point of where I have somebody at the office that's willing to take control of that.*

Carlos: What are the day to day challenges you face in running the business?

Joe Chavarria: *Day to day challenges? Making sure that the work is getting out on time. I mean that to me is probably the most important part of the day. Make sure that the team isn't dropping any work out. Now that I'm not involved so much I've given them the room to be able to do what they need to be doing. They understand their jobs and I expect them to get it done.*

entrepreneurs

Every now and then something gets dropped out and I'll have to kind of clean it up or I'll have to call or I'll have to go and see the customer and figure out how to make things right. Those are the times when I'll go back and explain to them what happened and what they need to be looking out for. It's all just experience.

Every Monday morning there are four things that I read to them. The same four statements that I make to them almost like our mantra. Number one is to read the work orders. And that means all the pages, all the notes, all the highlighted notes. I encourage them to take five or ten minutes if you have and make sure that they understand all of the information that's on the work order. They need to do that before starting any job. I let them know that I'd rather have them spend those five or ten minutes at the beginning of the job rather than using the wrong information, getting the job wrong and then having to re-order and re-print the job. That's way more expensive not just in terms of the cost of goods or labor, but also to our reputation. That's number one.

The second thing I tell them is to read their e-mails and respond. Because a lot of times even though there may be five or six people reading the e-mails that can answer a question sometimes they just read them and don't let anybody know there was a change or maybe they saw a mistake nobody else caught. So I try to get them to understand we all need to respond back with just a quick, hey I got your e-mail and we're going to send you artwork. They can't just let their email sit because it leaves the other person guessing.

<u>entrepreneurs</u>

The third thing I tell them is to ask questions, don't guess. If they're like me, if I have a 50/50 chance, I always guess wrong. That's why I ask the question and I encourage them to ask questions as well.

And then the last one is I ask them to write things down because you're not going to remember. That goes for everyone on the team including myself because sometimes I think I'll remember a small detail and then a couple of days go by and I forgot because I didn't write it down. Well the teams that are screen printing they have to write down the ink formulas; they have to write down the print order; they have to write down how they printed the job. And it's the same thing with the embroidery teams. They have to write down the thread colors because there may be a repeat order. And the next time they go to do that job if they don't have that information they're going to be guessing. They're going to have to call the customer who may or may not know what thread color it is specifically. It's just wasting time because now instead of moving forward on production you're taking another half hour just to get the information that you need. So those are the four things that I read to them every Monday morning.

Carlos: What do you think the biggest threat to your business is right now and how do you hedge against that??

Joe Chavarria: *No doubt it's the internet. It's the Amazons of the world. They are the ones millennials or now anyone really can get online and they can order today and it's at their doorstep tomorrow and there is the perception that screen printing is the same thing. In the short term we're protected somewhat because we are a custom order shop*

entrepreneurs

but to be honest with you it's not too far off in the future where Amazon or some of the larger printing companies are going to start offering custom screen printing or embroidery and the customer can have it within a couple of days shipped and delivered. So our competition isn't the local screen printers, or embroiderers, it's the internet.

So we just have to get better at how we do our work in terms of how we deliver; how we schedule; how we're receiving orders; how we're able to respond. It's one of the things that I tell our employees. We've got to be able to set up a job with no mistakes. Print the job with no mistakes, and then take it down and set the next job. By doing those small things right we can cut our lead times down.

If we can cut it down to a week, then I think we can combat losing business to Amazon. Because in the end a lot of our customers still like to be able to touch and feel and see before they order anything. That's where we have an edge over Amazon. We can give customers a physical sample of what they want which provides reassurance when they're about to buy 500 shirts for their kids soccer league. There's that fear that even if they can get the shirts in a couple of days, if the design is wrong or isn't what they expected they'll have to reorder everything. So now that we're getting this other auto press, then we'll have two auto presses that we'll be able to cut down our delivery time.

But it's an area of the business that we're constantly working on. That's why I say if we can be more efficient at our jobs it's going to make us more competitive. If I can get the teams to understand that if they take that extra five minutes before they print the job to read all of the information on the work order then they're not going to have

entrepreneurs

any issues. We're not going to have to go back and reprint which slows everything down and reduces our ability to serve our customers.

Carlos: So you mentioned you had a business partner originally. How did you get connected with him? Was he an investor you pitched an idea to? Or was he a relative?

Joe Chavarria: *Well he was a customer I had become friends with. He was always talking about starting up a business and he wanted to know if I would go in business with him. I wasn't certain how I felt about the partnership but to be honest with you it made it easier for me to start everything up because we were under-capitalized when we first opened. We didn't have any operating capital to speak of. I mean we just kind of got by on mostly my reputation. I had spent the time building relationships with people. I knew a lot of people in the industry that were either our vendors who sold the products or our customers in companies who were able to kind of opened me up with their companies. I was able to get a couple of them to give me some net thirty terms and we were able to manage and squeak by and build the business that way. So in the end it worked out a lot better than I had first imagined.*

Carlos: So, just kind of going back to what we talked about earlier, that kind of reinforces the idea that building those relationships with your vendors is critical. You had developed personal relationships and friendships with some of the reps and that's how you were kind of able to get started?

Joe Chavarria: *Yes. It is critical. Because they knew who I was from all of the purchasing I had done for the other company that I worked at. You have to be willing to stick*

entrepreneurs

your neck out there. You have to be willing to talk to these guys. You have to. That's how they know you. That's how they get to know your reputation as a company. Even when you're buying from them because believe me they talk amongst themselves. So if you're not doing what you're supposed to be doing like paying them back; they're going to hear about it. The other companies; all the reps talk to each other. So it was a big deal.

Carlos: If there's one thing you could tell yourself 14 years ago what would it be?

Joe Chavarria: *I probably should have looked at buying a building right away. No matter the cost. I should have looked at buying a building right away.*

Carlos: What advice do you have for other people who want to start a business, any business?

Joe Chavarria: *Make sure you research it. You've got to do your research. You have to look into the industry. Even if it's an industry that you already know about you still have to know what it's going to take for you to get started. Things like how are you going to get customers? What's your ideal state? How are you going to market yourself?*

Also you need to know your customer base. That's one of the things that I already knew when I started. I knew what my customer base was. I knew where I was going to go look for business. I wrote it down in my business plan that I actually took a lot of time and care to write up. Even though when I took it to the bank they didn't. They just read the front page and put it over to the side and asked me what I had for collateral. A big thorough business plan might be important for big time financing or an IPO or

entrepreneurs

something. For a new company seeking a small business loan, it's entirely about collateral. At least in my experience.
Carlos: What did you have for collateral?
Joe Chavarria: *Just the equity on my home. That was it.*
Carlos: So you risked everything. Did you have any doubts?
Joe Chavarria: *No. I didn't have any doubts. I knew it was going to work.*
Carlos: What did Mom think about all of it?
Joe Chavarria: *When we talked about it she really did just say well, we've been poor before. But she didn't really question me about any of the stuff. I think one of the things that I didn't really like take a lot of money out of the business in the beginning so she kind of supported us, and the business at times. I remember a couple of times where she had to loan the company money to pay a vendor. She was paid back, but it was a sacrifice. In the beginning, whenever I could get paid out of the company I would take a paycheck. It was enough for us to maintain and we were able to pay our bills.*
Carlos: There were times when you didn't take a paycheck from the company.
Joe Chavarria: *There are still times I don't take a paycheck. We're not spending our money as if there was no end to it. We kind of save and we're not out spending money every day or every weekend. We were a little bit more controlled than a lot of people. So that was never an issue. I mean even though we didn't have a lot of extra money, it was enough for us to get by.*

take away

entrepreneurs

Caring about people. My father embodies that belief and while he may not have emphasized this explicitly during the interview it's exactly what I identified and connected with immediately. Caring about people is a phrase often thrown around in business. Caring about employees; caring about customers; caring about people in the community. These are all things you'll find a lot of major corporations talking about. The success of my dad's business is 14 years of evidence that that supports the notion that these values, a caring attitude, does contribute to the success a business. Caring for people can be an effective trait leaders can utilize to enable success for themselves, and those around them.

I've often heard managers or leaders at companies talk about how they can't give away the farm. This is true. But for me, truly caring about a person in a professional setting isn't about giving away products or services to a customer, or not holding an employee accountable. Caring about people is foundational to building relationships with customers and with team members.

Caring about a team member may mean having tough conversations about things like attendance or performance. You're showing you care about their success. Caring about all your customers may mean firing your worst customers. Tim Ferriss popularized this idea in his book _The 4-hour Workweek_. Neither of those things may be fun or easy to do, especially if you do care about people. But in both cases if you know you've done your due diligence you can approach the situation with confidence that you're making the best decision for the

entrepreneurs

health of your business. For example allowing one person to continuously decline in performance can impact moral and therefore engagement for the rest of your team. Likewise allowing one toxic customer to dominate your time means less time to develop and foster healthy relationships with more agreeable clients.

    A key part to building his business into a success was my dad's ability to form, and maintain relationships with his customers. I related a story that happened around Christmas of 2017 where a complete stranger approached me on the basis of wearing a hoodie with my dad's logo on it. It resulted in a 10 minute conversation about how wonderful New Generation was, and how good they were in working in the community. And all of the praise, and compliments, and genuine excitement about a t-shirt company was centered around the relationship my dad had fostered with this individual, because he cares.

    One thing that strikes me so deeply about this incident is how unique a scenario this is. I'm a sports fan and have had a number of conversations about different teams or athletes with strangers in passing. There are also ubiquitous companies such as Amazon, Pepsi, Coke, and FedEx we all know and use. Nobody has ever approached me on the street for wearing a PepsiCo jacket (which I have) or a Frito-Lay shirt (which I also have). Both of those brands are clearly more recognizable than my dad's company. And sports teams in particular generate a lot of loyalty (particularly in Philadelphia. Go Eagles!) but aside from a few brief, "go Eagles" from a fan at an airport, I've never been stopped to discuss how wonderful Jeff Lurie is.

entrepreneurs

So what motivated this person to take time out of their day to strike up a conversation with a complete stranger over a local company? My dad built a relationship with that person because caring about people has been the foundation for my dad's success, and something he recognized as important to him as a person, and a value he focused on for how he chooses to run his business.

A year out from the interview I thought about what I had learned from my dad is how big of an impact relationship building has on the performance of those around you. In a leadership role your success often depends on the performance of your team. Showing you care can drive engagement and build a place that people enjoy working at.

When my dad said, *"you can enjoy your job,"* it had a big impact on me and the way I viewed not just leadership, but my career in general. I went from looking for a company I could work for, to a leader I could follow. A good leader can make the day to day of a job feel enjoyable, and that's what my dad tries to do. He knows his company isn't for everyone, and not everybody that works for him is going to become a millionaire. But they can enjoy their time there and leverage their experience to take onto the next stage of their journey.

entrepreneurs

closing

There are many different types of entrepreneurs, and many different types of businesses you can start. The above selection is only a small sliver of America, and the dream it represents for so many people. Not just the people who were lucky enough to be born here, but also people around the world. America is a beacon of hope and opportunity. It's important to remember that beacon is kept alight by the entrepreneurs who are living out their dreams now, and the future entrepreneurs who are working towards one day living that dream.

It's also important to remember is that there's no one set path to success and everyone's picture of success looks different. Even the picture of success you created today may change as your worldview changes. As a result the topics discussed about running a business and being a good leader may or may not be applicable to you. Maybe technology will drive out the need for your employees. Maybe you're your only employee and team building isn't that important to you (but you should definitely care about people including yourself). Maybe there is such a labor surplus you can act as a tyrannical dictator (please don't). Again, the goal was to present information that you could use to form your own leadership style, and develop a cadence that works for you. Whatever path you choose or goals you set I hope reading this helps make your journey a little smoother, and achieve your goals a little faster.

I hope you enjoyed reading these stories. I think it's important to give a voice to small business leaders particularly in an age where we see more and more

entrepreneurs

political rhetoric driving wedges into our community. Regardless of your political or religious ideologies business owners are people, and they are a part of your community. They are your neighbors, your friends, your loved ones. Your kids share the same schools, and the same streets. You shop at the same stores. And more than likely, you share the same dreams about your futures. I hope this book inspires you in some small way. To treat others better by caring about the people around you. To treat yourself better and find a career or job you can enjoy, and build healthy relationships with those around you. Maybe you'll be so inspired you'll take a leap and start your own business. Whatever it does I hope it helps you feel more connected to the world around you.

www.ingramcontent.com/pod-product-compliance
Lightning Source LLC
Chambersburg PA
CBHW072136170526
45158CB00004BA/1401